Fantasy, Forgery, and the Byron Legend

Fantasy,
Forgery,
and the
Byron Legend

JAMES SODERHOLM

THE UNIVERSITY PRESS OF KENTUCKY

Scholarly publisher for the Commonwealth,
serving Bellarmine College, Berea College, Centre
College of Kentucky, Eastern Kentucky University,
The Filson Club, Georgetown College, Kentucky
Historical Society, Kentucky State University,
Morehead State University, Murray State University,
Northern Kentucky University, Transylvania University,
University of Kentucky, University of Louisville,
and Western Kentucky University.

Editorial and Sales Offices:
The University Press of Kentucky
663 South Limestone Street, Lexington, Kentucky 40508–4008

frontispiece: Lord Byron, Thomas Phillips.
Newstead Abbey, Nottingham City Museums.

Library of Congress Cataloging-in-Publication Data
Soderholm, James, 1957–
  Fantasy, forgery, and the Byron legend / James Soderholm.
    p. cm.
  Includes bibliographical references and index.
  ISBN 0-8131-1939-1 (cloth : alk. paper)
  1. Byron, George Gordon Byron, Baron, 1788–1824—Authorship.
2. Byron, George Gordon Byron, Baron, 1788–1824—Relations with
women. 3. Poets, English—19th century—Biography—History and
criticism. 4. Literary forgeries and mystifications—History—19th
century. 5. Authors and readers—Great Britain—History—19th
century. 6. Women and literature—History—19th century. 7. Fame—
History—19th century. 8. Self in literature. I. Title.
PR4382.S63 1995
821'.7—dc20   95-17130

for Jerome McGann

Who loves, raves—'tis youth's frenzy—but the cure
  Is bitterer still; as charm by charm unwinds
  Which robed our idols, and we see too sure
  Nor worth nor beauty dwells from out of the mind's
  Ideal shape of such; yet still it binds
  The fatal spell, and still it draws us on,
  Reaping the whirlwind from the oft-sown winds;
  The stubborn heart, its alchemy begun,
Seems ever near the prize,—wealthiest when most undone.
          —Byron, *Childe Harold's Pilgrimage* 3.1099–1107

  Women are prone to judge their lovers' hearts
  But by their own, which little semblance hath
  With man's rough nature. Hence they love them for
  The qualities they give them—not for those
  They have, which rarely merit to be loved.
                              —Lady Blessington

Contents

Illustrations

Acknowledgments

I am grateful to the following journals for allowing me to reprint revised and expanded articles as chapters 2, 3, and 4: *Keats-Shelley Journal, The Byron Journal, Nineteenth-Century Contexts.*

Many thoughtful friends improved this work—and my mind—while I was in graduate school at the University of Virginia: Lyell Asher, Richard Begam, Anne Birberick, Jay Dobrutsky, Deborah Garfield, Barbara Green, Daniel Kinney, and Cecil Lang. Paul Cantor supported me both financially and intellectually and remembered to shake my hand and wish me well when I collected the Ph.D. Richard Rorty had kind words about this book when it was a dissertation. My more general debt to his way of thinking and writing is immeasurable. Donna Soderholm read the book just before it went to press and, as always, her open heart and mind encouraged me. Bill Soderholm, who first put me under the spell of words, gave the manuscript an editorial scrubbing I shall not soon forget. A bare sentence cannot depict my esteem for the pilgrim soul of Anatole Mori, who before my eyes became the better maker.

The book is dedicated to the most generous scholar I know.

A Note On Citations

Byron's Letters and Journals, 12 vols., ed. Leslie A. Marchand (London: John Murray, 1973–82). All quotations from the letters and journals are taken from this edition and cited in the text as *BLJ*, followed by volume and page number.

Lord Byron: The Complete Poetical Works, 7 vols., ed. Jerome J. McGann (Oxford: Clarendon Press, 1980–92). All quotations from the poetry will be from this edition and cited in the text as *CPW*, followed by volume and page number.

INTRODUCTION
The Grammar of Glamour

By a coincidence of labors—one literary, one maternal (but both Scottish)—the word "glamour" and George Gordon Byron came into the world at about the same time. Walter Scott and Robert Burns first gave the word "glamour" literary currency. Scott used it in his 1802 ballad "Christie's Will," in which a group of gypsies dupes a schoolmaster by magically entrapping him:

> He thought the warlocks o' the rosy cross
>> Had fang'd him in their nets sae fast;
> Or that the gipsies' glamour'd gang
>> Had laired his learning at the last.

In a note to this poem Scott glossed the folklore underpinning such a trick: "Besides the prophetic powers, ascribed to the gypsies in most European countries, the Scottish peasants believe them possessed of the power of throwing upon bystanders a spell, to fascinate their eyes, and cause them to see the thing that is not."[1] In his *Letters on Demonology and Witchcraft* (1830), Scott discussed this power of fascination ascribed to sorceresses and gave it a native habitation: "This species of Witchcraft is well known in Scotland as the glamour, or *deceptio visus,* and was supposed to be a special attribute of the race of Gypsies."[2]

As another example of this form of fascination, Scott cites "The Gypsie Laddie," a song in which enchantment and seduction work together.

> The gypsies came to our good lord's gate,
>> And wow but they sang sweetly;
> They sang sae sweet and sae very complete,
>> That down came the fair lady.

> And she came tripping down the stair,
>> And a' her maids before her;
> As soon as they saw her weel-far'd face,
>> They coost the glamer o'er her.

Under the spell of "the glamer," the Countess of Cassillis elopes with the gypsy leader, and the rest of the song recounts her capitulation to the powers that have seduced her.[3]

Still another important use of "glamour" appears in Scott's *Lay of the Last Minstrel* (1805). Happening upon the magic book entrusted to the wounded William of Deloraine, a goblin-dwarf tries to pry it open.

> The iron band, the iron clasp,
> Resisted long the elfin grasp:
> For when the first he had undone,
> It closed as he the next begun.
> Those iron clasps, that iron band,
> Would not yield to unchristened hand,
> Till he smeared the cover o'er
> With the Borderer's curdled gore;
> A moment then the volume spread,
> And one short spell therein he read,
> It had much of glamour might,
> Could make a ladye seem a knight;
> The cobwebs on a dungeon wall
> Seem tapestry in lordly hall;
> A nut-shell seem a gilded barge,
> A sheeling seem a palace large,
> And youth seem age, and age seem youth—
> All was delusion, naught was truth. [Canto 3, stanza 9]

The might of "the glamour" allows the dwarf to become a shape-shifting deceiver, much like Morgan le Fay of Arthurian legend. In Scott's works, then, glamour is associated with the power to create illusions, derived in this instance from a book of spells.

Robert Burns also introduced a literary usage of the word "glamour" in his "On the Late Captain Grose's Peregrinations thro' Scotland, collecting the Antiquities of that Kingdom" (1789).

Ilk ghaist that haunts auld ha' or chamer,
Ye gipsy-gang that deal in glamor,
And you, deep-read in hell's black grammar,
    Warlocks and Witches;
Ye'll quake at his conjuring hammer,
    Ye midnight b——es. [ll. 19–24]

Burns makes an explicit connection between supernatural deal-
ings in "glamour" and the special knowledge of language
("Hell's black grammar") from which this power derives. The
genealogy that connects a scholastic conception of grammar to
the gypsy practice of deception shows us the history of this in-
triguing word.

In classical Greek and Latin, the word [grammar] denoted the method-
ological study of literature in the widest sense, including textual and
aesthetic criticism, investigation of literary history and antiquities,
explanation of allusions, etc., besides the study of Greek and Latin
languages. Post-classically, grammatica came to be restricted to the
linguistic portion of this discipline, and eventually to "grammar" in
the modern sense. In the Middle Ages, grammatica and its Roman
forms chiefly meant the knowledge or study of Latin, and were hence
used as synonymous with learning in general, the knowledge peculiar
to the learned classes. As this was popularly supposed to include
magic and astrology, the Old French *gramaire* was sometimes used as
a name for these occult sciences. In these applications it still survives
in certain corrupt forms, F. *grimoire*, Eng. *Glamour, Gramarye*).[4]

In his *Intellectual Systems* (1678), Ralph Cudworth alludes
to grammar's astral meaning: "They who are skilled in the
Grammar of the Heavens may be able to spell out future
Events." Dante's version of this celestial grammar appears in
Canto 18 of the *Paradiso*, where the "holy creatures" form
"five times seven vowels and consonants" and write a proverb
from the *Book of Wisdom*. Milton also seems to have had this
sense of grammar in mind in *Paradise Regained* (1671): "By
what stars in their conjunction met, give me to spell" (4.385).
The difference is that these heavenly writings have nothing to
do with deception and everything to do with enlightenment, or
at least prescience. From Milton to Burns one jumps from a

quasi-religious view of grammar to a body of folklore that associates it with the enchantments and deceptive conjurings of gypsies. When Burns rhymes "glamour" with "grammar," then, he has more than his ear guiding him, for the medieval sense of grammar had evidently worked itself into Scottish folklore, connected by the practice of reading spells and casting them.

One wonders how we moved from the sense of "glamour" bequeathed to us by Scottish folklore to our modern sense of the word, where glamour tends to be only skin deep.[5] At the end of the nineteenth century, authors were still drawing on the Scottish sense of the word. In "Enid" (1859), for example, Tennyson appeals to medieval legends and writes of "that maiden in the tale, / Whom Gwydion made by glamour out of flowers."[6] Similarly, in *Cleopatra* (1889), H. Rider Haggard describes a scene in which the magician Harmachis impresses the queen with his illusions: "In a little while the place, to their glamoured sight, was a seething sea of snakes, that crawled, hissed, and knotted themselves in knots."[7] Only in this century has the magic associated with glamour given way to a more colloquial and commercial use of the word.[8]

Some modern dictionaries still note the occult sense of glamour first, before going on—as *Webster's Third New International Dictionary* does—to the entries "glamour boy—a man (as an actor or adventurer) with whom glamour is esp. associated"; "glamour girl—a woman (as an actress or model) with whom glamour is esp. associated"; and "glamour puss," which it recognizes as slang and glosses, again tautologically, as "one who has a glamorously attractive face."[9] The magical practice of casting the "glamourye" over one's victim has slipped into the night of antiquated folklore, for now we typically view glamour as a trick of cosmetics, the *deceptio visus* of a rouged visage or a deceptively alluring "glamour puss." Interestingly enough, we now call such glamour pusses "stars," and we are still infatuated with reading (about) them.

The word "glamour" has, then, passed through three distinct but related stages. It first referred to a bedazzling illusion cast upon somebody by gypsies or wizards and was associated with an occult knowledge of spells. Glamour then came to mean an inner aura that magically enchants those in its vicinity, a power we now call "charisma." Today, glamour can be purchased and put on like makeup, and both men and women "buy into" what might be called "applied aura." The special knowledge one once needed to deal in glamour, the ability to read and cast spells, now involves knowing how to read advertising copy. More important, however, is the fact that glamour has become not an enchantment a magician casts over victims to bedazzle their sight, but rather an enchantment one can, quite literally, apply to oneself.

In Byron's life and legend we see the modern and antiquated senses of glamour overlap. He was (and is) a "glamour boy" who borrows not a little of his seductive magic from those who would touch—and touch up—their idol. In demystifying this spell we recognize that both forms of glamour are partly the result of public investment and invention. As much phenomenon as artifact, "Byron" was half-perceived and half-created. Unlike Wordsworth, Byron was often a man writing to women, some of whom wrote back and invested the poet with great significance. This is not surprising to learn, but the details of some of these investments have often been ignored or sentimentalized in order to subdue their complexity.

In this study I examine well-known and generally unknown writings of five women—Elizabeth Pigot, Caroline Lamb, Annabella Milbanke, Teresa Guiccioli, and Marguerite Blessington—who participated in Byron's life, literary career, and legend.[10] I offer these chapters as a contribution to the reception history of Byron's works and as revisionist biographical criticism, a mode of inquiry in which authors, poems, letters, forgeries, journals, and conversations so variously intersect that it sometimes becomes difficult to see where one subject (both "topic" and "agent") leaves off and another begins.

Like Oscar Wilde, Byron was, as Ralph Milbanke (Earl of Lovelace and Byron's grandson) put it, "curiously addicted to imitating anything that might impress him as a literary image of himself."[11] He might have added that this addiction was general all over England and intensified by a Byronic exhibitionism that drew many into its motions and routines. Annabella Milbanke, Byron's wife for one disastrous year, diagnosed this cultish activity and called it "Byromania," a phenomenon that flourished even—or, rather, especially—after Byron died. Reconstructing contemporary receptions and reproductions of Byron's works is a good way to explore the emergence of a mode of literary fame, a contest of englamoured images in which the fanciful and the real are lost in the veils of soulmaking.

Near the end of his life, Byron would reflect upon these rituals of enchantment when he wrote *Don Juan*.

> His manner was perhaps the more seductive,
>   Because he ne'er seem'd anxious to seduce;
> Nothing affected, studied, or constructive
>   Of coxcombry or conquest: no abuse
> Of his attractions marr'd the fair perspective,
>   To indicate a Cupidon broke loose,
> And seem to say, "resist us if you can"—
> Which makes a dandy while it spoils a man.
> [*CPW* 5:592]

In Don Juan, Byron naturalizes the artificiality of "coxcombry or conquest" and thus solves the problem of constructed appearances, those abusive affectations that form dandies and cult figures but spoil men.

Yet it is precisely through sexual enchantment that both Byron and Juan become complexly "made" men, Cupidons loosed from the moorings of truth, sincerity, and authenticity who produce—and are produced by—seductive texts. Of Juan we also learn that

> his manner was his own alone:
> Sincere he was—at least you could not doubt it,
>   In listening merely to his voice's tone.
> The Devil hath not in all his quiver's choice
> An arrow for the heart like a sweet voice. [*CPW* 5:592]

Byron bestows his own devilishly "sweet voice," the voice of sincerity, on Juan—the son he never had. In Juan's presumably unconstructed demeanor, Byron presents an inverted fantasy image of his carefully fashioned poetic/erotic persona. Juan's cagey passivity offers bashfulness and candor as seductive arts whereby one can be "insinuating without insinuation" (*CPW* 5:593), the very arts that serve Byron as a poetic seducer who delights in deception, innuendo, and subterfuge, as an ingenious coxcomb who constructs images of himself—including the image of his sincerity—to beguile his readers.

By the time he wrote *Don Juan*, however, Byron recognized that women also create the illusions at the heart of seduction. What the narrator of *Don Juan* says of the hero might be said with equal accuracy of the poet:

> with women he was what
> They pleased to make or take him for; and their
> Imagination's quite enough for that:
> So that the outline's tolerably fair,
> They fill the canvass up—and "verbum sat."
> If once their phantasies be brought to bear
> Upon an object, whether sad or playful,
> They can transfigure brighter than a Raphael. [*CPW* 5:593]

Byron understood, as Jean Baudrillard observes, that "to seduce is to die as reality and reconstitute oneself as illusion."[12] A seducer and a poet, Byron regularly died in order to remake himself, or rather to make himself up. But several readers met him at least halfway in this enchanted activity. Their fantasies and fictions constructed Byron according to their various ambitions and generated a series of self-deceptions and self-seductions that relied on the power of illusion and the love of death and (self-)transfiguration.

Indeed, the activities and writings surrounding Byron's legend constitute an important moment in the history of renown, a moment when a cult figure found his name and fame possessed by those who first enshrined him, when his works became public property, when his authorship and authority

were challenged and his fame democratized. This moment can
be fairly accurately dated. In Byron's immensely popular nar-
rative poem *The Corsair* (1814), Medora gazes in wonder at the
pirate of her dreams and asks a question that thousands of
English and Continental readers would ask of their attraction
to the author: "What sudden spell hath made this man so
dear?" Byron's success in manipulating his poetic images in
conjunction with and as reflections of his public image ac-
counts for much of his glamour, but the spell that made him
so alluring had much to do with his readers' own investment
in the poet's life and career. Fame and glamour often result
from complex acts of representation in which a cult figure and
those who "cultivate" him join fanciful forces. Although
Byron enjoyed toying with those who took seriously his fic-
tional—and sexual—personae, he was unprepared for the kinds
of responses his legend and his writings would generate. Be-
cause of the desire to participate in the life and fame of one's
hero, and the will to do so in writing, Byron awoke in 1812 to
find himself not only famous but also drawn into the fray of
fantasy and forgery, activities over which he had little control.

About one hundred years after the publication of *The Cor-
sair*, Ethel Colburn Mayne asked and presumed to answer
Medora's question: "What *was* the secret of his spell? . . .
Personal glamour is the only answer to that eternal question: a
degree of personal glamour which, it is not too much to say, has
never been possessed by anyone else in the world."[13] For Mayne
in 1905, it was precisely Byron's unrivaled "personal glamour"
that made the spell of his personality so strong.[14] In the only
book-length study on the women associated with the poet,
Margot Strickland writes that, "confronted by a Byron, women
do not react logically, but biologically."[15] The terms of this as-
sertion certainly need revision, particularly since not all women
swooned over—or even admired—Byron. It is worth noting, for
example, that some of his female contemporaries had almost no
reaction. In a letter to her sister Cassandra, Jane Austen wrote:
"I have read the Corsair, mended my petticoat, & have nothing
else to do."[16] As if by osmosis, on the other hand, Edward Tre-

lawny absorbed and became *The Corsair*, a copy of which he kept under his pillow.[17] S.T. Coleridge's excited confession that he never saw so lovely a countenance as Byron's reverberates in Frederic Raphael's claim in 1982 that "there is something beyond mundane analysis in the glamour of Lord Byron."[18] Arguing that Byron enjoys a mythic status, Raphael associates his legend with that of Oedipus and Dionysos. Byron's "unique glamour," then, transcends the ordinary because he "belongs to the world of myth."[19] Raphael's excitement about Byron's glamour puts him in league with a fan such as Trelawny and suggests that treating the poet as a cult object is not a particularly gendered phenomenon, either in his time or in our own. For Raphael, Byron's glamour has archetypal, even metaphysical proportions. More recently Camille Paglia has characterized Byron as "an Alcibiades whose glamour was too intense for his own society."[20] Yet Mayne, Raphael, and Paglia fail to explore the secret of Byron's magnetism by returning to the joint conjurings, occult learning, image-making, and seductions associated with "glamour" in its original sense. I hope to illumine these deceptions and enchantments by presenting five increasingly complicated case studies in Byromania.

Byron's literary relations with women began in provincial Southwell, where he met the young Elizabeth Pigot, who encouraged him to circulate his early poetry and to this end often produced fair copies of his writings. Biographers ignore key elements of their poetic and epistolary exchanges in order to simplify and sentimentalize her importance to him. Their most telling literary exchange appears in the margins of a book they had read, where Pigot challenged Byron's flattering deceits, and where he responded in kind with his first hearty exercise in self-conscious hypocrisy. He presented himself as the instrument of candor, praising those physical perfections he magically, if conventionally, concocts. But apparently Pigot did make herself the referent of some of his erotic poems. In doing this she prefigured a whole series of women who caught and communicated Byromania and its cultish representations.

Pigot's kind offices involved responding to Byron's Ovidian seductions, but she also became his first confidante and a "rational companion" to whom he could disclose some of his deepest secrets. Pigot's companionship, then, consisted not merely in her activities as Byron's faithful amanuensis, a copier of his poems, but also as the first woman who knew how to *read* him, how to decode his encodings. The coded talk in his letters to Pigot shows not only the depth of Byron's trust but also his confidence that she would be able to read the grammar of his self-enchantments and yet not take his erotic illusions too seriously. She wrote little to or about Byron, yet she had a hand in the construction of his social and poetic personality. Her interest in his private life and the way he mishandled his social image made her a critical, if ultimately benign, reader of his early career.

After Byron became famous, many women treated him as a love idol modeled on the antiheroes from his fiction. Caroline Lamb, for example, fell in love with *Childe Harold's Pilgrimage* and Childe Harold, and made the mistake of equating the author of the former with the constructed personality of the latter—a connection Byron took some pains to repudiate, even though he encouraged the identification when it suited his purposes. Lamb spent several years succumbing to his literary images, but she finally grew sick of them and of Byron's "moments of gloom, careworn brows, mysterious personages, marble hearts and the whole of that which had deceived her and many others."[21] She avenged herself on those who made her a hysterical figure by writing a roman à clef called *Glenarvon*. When told of Lamb's depiction of him in it, Byron archly observed: "It seems to me that, if the authoress had written the *truth* and nothing but the truth—the whole truth,—the romance would not only have been more *romantic*, but more entertaining. As for the likeness, the picture can't be good—I did not sit long enough"[*BLJ* 5:131].

Byron believed that his love affairs did not need touching up, that the truths of his romantic life were more interesting than anything the imagination could invent. But he enjoyed entwining truth and fiction, especially in his romantic adventures, and Lamb deftly plagiarized his spell by creating her own Byronic antihero. Between 1812 and 1814, however, one cannot tell the sorcerer from the eager apprentice, Narcissus from Echo. Indeed, by forging a letter to herself from Byron in order to obtain Byron's favorite picture of himself, known as the Newstead miniature, she quite literally and literarily spelled trouble for him, threatening his authority and undermining his desire to keep his affairs private. For a few hexed months, Lamb and Byron took turns bewitching each other. Both conjured up images, deceits, and forgeries in order to rival each other's most potent fantasies.

Sensing the resemblance that one "Byron" bore to the Gothic villains of his oriental tales, Annabella Milbanke then tried to make this fallen spirit over in her own semi-sacred image and to break the marble heart that had beguiled her peers. She wrote a poem, "The Byromania," to attack the female cult that Byron's "magic sway" had seduced. In an attempt to avoid what she saw as a slavish complicity with Byron's self-representations, Milbanke tried to reconstruct him. Her unpublished poetry shows how far she went to bring about his salvation. It also indicates how Byron's gloomy brow excited her imagination, drawing her into an alliance with his worshipers. Her participation in Byron's cult of images culminated in a poem in which she assumed the voice of "Thyrza," the young girl (in real life a young man—the Cambridge chorister John Edleston) whom Byron commemorated in a number of elegies. This was Milbanke's most hypnotic poem, and it represents one of the most peculiar contributions to the Byron legend. Although Byron did solicit her reformations during their engagement, he eventually divorced himself from images that were meant to save his soul.

Teresa Guiccioli's thoroughgoing attempt to forge a new Byron continued the work Milbanke had begun. More than any of her predecessors, Guiccioli involved herself in Byron's poetic career. Her work as both editor and copier of some of his later poems and her efforts to chasten and morally salvage him made her the second of his great spiritualizers. Her *Lord Byron jugé par les témoins de sa vie* (1869, published anonymously and posthumously), based on her epic biography *La vie de Byron en Italie*, dematerializes Byron, and her editing and selective citation technique effectively unwrite the body—and the bawdyness—of his poetry. Her claim to have spoken with Byron's spirit in séances, and the automatic writing these sessions occasioned, demonstrated that her Byromania spanned the grave and granted her sole copyright to Byron's very spirit. These sessions represented the apogee of self-seduction, as Guiccioli joined Byron's phantom voice to her fantasy image of him. Her genius for conjuring up a Catholic Byron after his death fulfilled her lifelong ambition to sanctify his poetic images and his personal reputation. In acting as the medium for his spiritual transmission, she invented her own grammar of glamour, raised the stakes of Byromania, and pioneered the first biographical transfiguration of Byron.

Marguerite Blessington published her conversations with Byron eight years after his death. Her Boswellizing exploited the popularity of an emerging literary mode—gossip; her series of interviews also foreshadows a modern obsession with the vices of celebrities. And yet her depiction of Byron's many faces and poses reflects her own social chameleonism. That Byron was studying Blessington for his portrayal of the shape-shifting Adeline in the English cantos of *Don Juan* makes it difficult to tell who is the subject of whom. If Lamb forged Byron's hand, Blessington framed him while conjuring up the fearless symmetries of their personalities; her particular genius consisted in analyzing Byron's personality even as she presented many of her own views and idiosyncrasies. Her attempt to deglamorize the poet relied on sinuous deceptions, acts of mirroring, and elaborately constructed appearances: the stock-in-trade of Byronic illusion-making.

This study attempts to put the poet directly before certain members of his public and to see just what they made of him.[22] When in 1819 Byron wrote to John Murray, his London publisher, that "your Blackwood accuses me of treating women harshly—it may be so—but I have been their martyr.—My whole life has been sacrificed *to* them & *by* them" (*BLJ* 6:257), he was, in his usual half-facetious way, telling two important truths: that he had often been a moral monster in his relations with women; and that many women wielded great power over him, the power to make or break him, as one builds and then topples any idol. The following case studies recover the several contexts in which Byron's poetry enchanted certain readers who, by "martyring" him in their own writings, returned the favor.

The desire to participate in the life and fame of one's hero, and the will to do so, in writing, makes Byron a "made" man— and a marked (up) man—overnight. He awoke in 1812 not only to find himself famous but to find himself exposed, perhaps overexposed, and he spent the rest of his life responding to the effects of his literary mesmerization. These complex effects allow us to explore the joint conjurings, hoaxes, hexes, and self-deceptions animating the Byron legend. In these literary dramas we discover a sexualized agon[23] through which that legend regenerates itself in a succession of fantasy images, a "glamour industry." The main work of this industry involves reinvesting old images with new life or perhaps finding new ways of telling the story of the contemporary responses to Byron and his works. It involves participating in rituals of enchantment, those creative acts by which, as Childe Harold enticingly puts it, "we endow / With form our fancy, gaining as we give / The life we image" (*CPW* 2:78). These words sing an incantation, a spell that binds readers to the possibility of transfiguring themselves in and through the Byron they image and imagine. Jerome Christensen demystifies these rituals by putting them in commercial terms: "We gain as we give and only as we give: the commodity yields a profit on investment, but successful venture capitalism demands a continual reinvestment in the image, which maps a string of new and improved images."[24]

But the durability of the Byron legend also depends on a heavy traffic of conspicuously unimproved images: the literary production of anti-Byromania. Lady Blessington expertly created both improved and demeaning images of Byron for her reading public and indeed this yielded her a profit. Her work shows that there is more than one way to reinvest and circulate images. In passing out snapshots of Byron, she circulated miniatures of him in a way he found alternately exhilarating and vexing when Caroline Lamb did it more substantially with his prized Newstead portrait. By the time Blessington published her *Conversations*, however, Byron was no longer there to re-appropriate his preferred images and control the ways in which the fanciful and the real intermingled in reproducing him. After his death there was more and more room in the "discourse" of the Byron legend for possible subjects. Guiccioli's hagiographical treatment and especially her spiritual communion with him brought personal fantasy to bear on a poet who had become nothing more than an object, or pretext, for the imagination's transfiguring power. Guiccioli cast "the glamorye" on herself, and the dead poet miraculously immaterialized before her, canonized by her love. Like Blessington, she invested his public image and poetic images with her own likeness, writing his life and gaining (by) it at the same time.

Elizabeth Pigot. Silhouette in private hands.

1

Trial Fantasies:
Byron and Elizabeth Pigot

Elizabeth Bridget Pigot was a young lady living in provincial Southwell when Lord Byron arrived on the scene in the spring of 1804. She was twenty-one years old and Byron sixteen. The first woman involved with Byron in literary matters, Pigot won favor with him by copying out his early poems and by avoiding the conjugal intrigues of her peers. In her kind offices Byron found the encouragement he needed to grow into a combination of Anacreon, Ovid, Werther, and Thomas Moore. After 1808, Pigot, who lived to be eighty-three, never saw or heard from Byron again. She would write little to or about him, but their handful of letters and poems contain the germ of a cult of image worship, deception, and glamour that would make Byron a popular idol and his followers part of a general "Byromania."

In a letter to his half-sister Augusta dated April 9, 1804, Byron disports himself as the disaffected playboy of Southwell and mentions the party where he met Elizabeth Pigot.

My mother Gives a *party* tonight at which the principal *Southwell Belles* will be present, with one of which although I don't as yet know whom I shall so far *honour having never seen* them, I intend to *fall violently* in love, it will serve as an amusement pour passer le temps and it will at least have the charm of novelty to recommend it, then you know in the course of a few weeks I shall be quite au desespoir, shoot myself and Go out of the world with eclat, and my History will furnish materials for a pretty little Romance which shall be entitled and denominated the loves of Lord B. and the cruel and Inconstant Sigismunda Cunegunda Bridgetina &c&c princess of Terra Incognita.—Don't you think that I have a very Good Knack for *novel writing*? [*BLJ* 1:48]

The collection of "Southwell Belles" foreshadows all the women, fictional and real, who—Byron lavishly complained—persecuted him with their fickleness and deceit. He responded to them in a similar fashion. His next letter to Augusta, written about six months later, suggests how far down this path he had ventured: "I feel a little inclined to laugh at you, for love in my humble opinion, is utter nonsense, a mere jargon of compliments, romance, and deceit; now for my part had I fifty mistresses, I should in the course of a fortnight, forget them all, and if by chance I ever recollected one, should laugh at it as a dream, and bless my stars, for delivering me from the hands of the little mischievous Blind God" (*BLJ* 1:52).

Few youths have ever sounded so old, so roundly condescending, and so precociously detached. Wanting to pass himself off to Augusta as a sixteen-year-old citizen of the world, a man already beyond feeling who self-consciously scripts his emotions, Byron truffled his letters with à la mode idioms and recognized his own literary lovemaking for what it was: "a mere jargon of compliments." He continued to cultivate this verbal dandyism, especially in his later correspondence with Lady Melbourne, who helped him intermix his love and literary affairs.[1] But the letter above also gives us the words of a boy who knew something of disappointment and who tried to make light of romantic attachments by leavening them with irony.

Pigot's version of Byron's actual appearance and demeanor at the party in April shows how a touch of social reality dispatches his confident self-images. Biographers from Thomas Moore to Leslie Marchand and Willis Pratt have cited Pigot's account of her introduction to Southwell's little Ovid.

The first time I was introduced to him was at a party at his mother's, when he was so shy that she was forced to send for him three times before she could persuade him to come into the drawing-room, to play with the young people at a round game. He was then a fat bashful boy, with his hair combed straight over his forehead, and extremely like a miniature picture that his mother had painted by M. de Chambruland.[2]

Most portraits of Byron—and there were many—merely flatter him. In recording her impressions of the fat, bashful Byron,

Pigot did no more than describe the countenance "extremely like a miniature picture" that his mother had commissioned. But her account of Byron's appearance at the time of this party undoes the portrait of the gallant he presented in this letter to Augusta and thus renders an image (his "miniature" reputation) contrary to his own self-fashionings.

This same sobriety made her flinch when Byron's representations of her became equally glamorous, and he grew to honor her gravity. In one of his last letters to her, Byron acknowledged what Pigot meant to him.

Southwell, I agree with your Brother, is a *damned* place, I have done with it, & shall see it no more, (at least in all probability) excepting yourself, I esteem no one within its precincts, you were my only *rational* companion, & in plain truth I had more respect for you, than the whole *Bevy*, with whose foibles I *amused* myself in compliance with their *prevailing propensities*, you gave yourself more trouble with me & my *manuscripts*, than a thousand *dolls* would have done, believe me, I have not forgotten your good nature, in *this Circle of Sin*, & one day I trust shall be able to evince my gratitude.—As for the village *"Lass'es"* of *every description*, My *Gratitude* is also unbounded, to be equalled only by my *contempt*, I saw the *designs* of all *parties*, while they imagined me *every thing* to be *wished*. [*BLJ* 1:131]

This tribute suggests that Pigot's value to Byron consisted in her copying his poetry and not having any conjugal designs on him. Her rational demeanor kept her from folly and intemperance, although she sometimes delighted in making herself the recipient of some of Byron's erotic poems. Biographers typically fasten on all the beautiful images associated with this former role and mostly ignore or sentimentalize the implications and nuances contained in Pigot's desire to be on the receiving end of Byron's versified amorousness. To put it another way, biographers often take up with the very "prevailing propensities" of the Southwell bevy which Byron found so amusing. This continuity of representation suggests the complicity of later biographers in the image industry that Byron, or "Byronism," generates. We must think Pigot fair but not sexually enamored or intriguing, when perhaps the opposite was true.

Pigot may have been the only woman near Byron's own age to whom he could confide his actual, as opposed to his fantastical, desires. He sometimes repaid her clearheadedness by celebrating her plain looks in his early poetic idealizations, and by using his flattering arts to produce impossibly lovely images of her. One of Byron's most beguiling trial enchantments appears in a literary transaction with Pigot. Their exchange can be found in the margins of a book they read together, *Letters of an Italian Nun and an English Gentleman: Translated from the French of J.J. Rousseau.*[3] On the back flyleaf of this work, Pigot wrote a quatrain:

> Away, Away—your flattering arts,
> May now betray some simpler hearts,
> And *you* will *smile* at their believing,
> And *they* shall *weep* at your deceiving. [*CPW* 1:131]

This seems to have been written as much to the "English Gentleman" as to Byron, both of whom use flattering arts to "betray some simpler hearts." But Pigot's short poem underlines her own prescience. Byron's life, particularly his amorous life in Regency society, was a long trail of flattery, betrayal, and deception, a web of deceits that ensnared a number of women as well as Byron himself.

Inside the front cover of the Rousseau book Pigot also wrote a note: "In July 1804, this book was read by Ld Byron & he wrote in the fly leaf those lines which are printed in this first vol: of Poems, page 29—I was young & foolish then & was ashamed of them & tore them out.—I repent now—like many other people, when it is '*too late*'—E P—1834."[4] She is referring to page 29 of Byron's second privately printed volume, his *Poems on Various Occasions* (1807), which included the poem from the missing front flyleaf of the Rousseau book. Byron's response to Pigot's quatrain of charges mingles candor, flattery, and poetic deception; it thus foreshadows the poet's later exercises in fully self-conscious erotic spells.

> Dear simple girl those flattering arts,
> (From which you'd guard frail female hearts,)

Exist but in imagination,
Mere phantoms of your own creation;
For he who sees that witching grace,
That perfect form, that lovely face;
With eyes admiring, oh! believe me,
He never wishes to deceive thee;
Once let you at your mirror glance,
You'll there descry that elegance,
Which from our sex demands such praises,
But envy in the other raises.—
Then he who tells you of your beauty,
Believe me only does his duty;
Ah! fly not from the candid youth,
It is not flattery, but truth. [*CPW* 1:131]

In a later defense of his erotic lyrics, Byron essentially repeated to the Reverend John Becher (a Vicar of Nottingham who tried to discourage Byron's amorous versifying) the claim that concludes his response to Pigot: "The artless Helicon, I boast, is Youth; / My Lyre, the Heart;—my Muse, the simple Truth" (*CPW* 1:98).[5] But even as he makes a phantom of his alleged deception, Byron's flattering arts—his own version of an Ovidian *ars amatoria*—come to life in his lines to Pigot, who was by most accounts rather plain. The "perfect form" and "lovely face" Byron praises are precisely phantoms of *his* own creation, "exist[ing] but in imagination." It is his glamorizing of Pigot that transforms her ordinary features into a perfectly ideal loveliness and makes her a fit subject for his celebratory verse. Thus, "that witching grace" refers less to her perfect features than to the characteristic idealizations mirrored in the poetry itself.

The poem's rhetoric idealizes both Byron and Pigot in order to rebut the personal charge of false flattery. His flattery of her enacts the lie it disavows. To use the terms of his later poetry, he is "lying like truth" (*CPW* 3:177), practicing the art of deception and flattery that has brought him to pose as "the dupe of every smiling maid" even as he casts his "glamour-eye" over them. Writing on Byron's debt to the Della Cruscan mode of sentimental poetry, Jerome McGann observes that this myth of failed love, epitomized in the lyrics addressed to Susan Vaughan

(for example, in "Again deceived! again betrayed!"*CPW* 3:3),
generates "a work which once again deceives and betrays senti-
mental love by its pretenses to faithfulness and candor."[6] The
poem to Pigot, whose author is merely a "candid youth," does
nearly the same thing. An actual, average-looking girl, Pigot is
the antitype of Manfred's Astarte, a conjured female spirit who
represents the ideal of Byron's poetic imagination, a true phan-
tom of his own creation. If this early poem is a conscious
self-deception (or an advertised pretense), then it presents
Byron's reflections on the essential falseness of this kind of
poetry. The purpose of this poetry, McGann argues, "is to reveal
that body of falsehood, to expose the lies which the mind
through its imagination conjures up."[7] Judging by her reaction,
Pigot saw the poem as a clot of lies, less an exposure of falsehood
than a purposeful use of it. Unlike the Countess Cassillis in the
ballad "Johnie Faa," Pigot was not seduced by the glamorized
version of her that Byron's lyre sang to life. I suspect that she
later repented tearing out the poem not because she came to see
the justice of its encomium but because Byron achieved such
fame that even his bagatelles were treasured.

Pigot did not balk at Byron's conventionally charming early
poetry when its terms suited her. Indeed, she sometimes en-
joyed making herself the referent of his lyric lovemaking.
Byron may have written two more poems to Pigot, both enti-
tled "To M.S.G.," but we have only her testimony: a note on
her fair copy of the first says "G.G.B. to E.P." These poems may
originally have been addressed to one of three principal Marys,
and then retitled to propitiate Southwell prudery. One can see
from the Anacreonic effusions of the following poem why Pigot
would want to be its subject.

1.

Whene'er I view those lips of thine,
   Their hue invites my fervent kiss;
Yet, I forego that bliss divine,
   Alas! it were—unhallow'd bliss.

2.

Whene'er I dream of that pure breast,
    How could I dwell upon its snows;
Yet, is the daring wish represt,
    For that,—would banish its repose.

3.

A glance, from thy soul-searching eye,
    Can raise with hope, depress with fear;
Yet, I conceal my love, and why?
    I would not force a painful tear.

4.

I ne'er have told my love, yet thou
    Hast seen my ardent flame, too well;
And shall I plead my passion, now,
    To make thy bosom's heaven, a hell? [*CPW* 1:154]

The rest of the poem continues to argue the bewitching effect of declared love, especially for the recipient, who then would suffer the reproaches of the Southwell matrons. Whether Byron wrote this poem to Pigot we cannot know, but the evidence of *her* hand, both in making a fair copy and in stating that the poem was originally addressed to her, suggests that she at least wanted to be the poem's subject. When the terms of a poem suited her, she did not shrink from addressing it to herself. The poems she copied out in her own hand and directed to herself were her fair copies, just as they were fashioned as fairer copies of her. Thus, she eventually allowed Byron to put her under the spell of his poetry, but with little consequence for either of them; Pigot's fantasy of self-attribution began and ended with her. The desire to be the referent of Byron's love poems, however, intensified after he became famous: several women tried either to pin Byron down on his references or to fancy themselves imaged in his poetry and therefore—so goes the myth—in his heart.

The written evidence of Pigot's own hand hints at her relations with Byron, but again, biographical treatment of this material thins it out. Her only other surviving poem to Byron appears beneath the quatrain cited earlier. Since it appears on the same end flyleaf, Pratt assumes that Pigot wrote it: that they "seem to be in Elizabeth's hand, as if they were written at the same time as the others, may indicate that Elizabeth's feeling for her youthful friend was more romantic than has generally been thought."[8]

> These times are past, our Joy's are gone
> You leave me, leave this happy Vale;
> These Scenes I must retrace alone,
> Without *Thee*, what will they avail?
> Who can conceive, who has not proved,
> The anguish of a Last Embrace?
> When torn from all you fondly loved,
> You bade a long Adieu To Peace.

Such verses indicate that Pigot did feel strongly about Byron, though she was put off by his amorous overtures when they included praising her beauty.

Pratt quotes this poem, but no sooner does he broach the idea of a romantic attachment between Byron and Pigot than he qualifies it by pointing out that the only marked passage in the *Letters of an Italian Nun and an English Gentleman* "is probably a key to Elizabeth's feelings."[9] Pratt does not consider the possibility that Byron could have marked this passage, which appears in one of Isabella's letters to Mr. Croli:

The sincerity of affection is not proved by wild and incoherent declamation. Pure solid love is ever accompanied with reason; and, though its language may glow with more than common animation, though to common observers, it may appear sometimes to stray from its associate, it never quits in reality, that sober guidance which can alone preserve it from folly and intemperance.[10]

Pratt omits the following sentence: "If you imagine that the affections of a reasonable woman are to be gained by unmanly sensibility, you are shamefully mistaken."[11] The prudent reply of this "reasonable woman" is the model—Pratt's *biographical* model—for Pigot's character, and as a clue to her feelings it supersedes even the passionate lyric she wrote on the book's fly-leaf. Pratt's Pigot thus responds to Byron's "flattering arts" in the same way that Rousseau's Italian nun responds to the English gentleman's amorous overtures. This passage from Rousseau, according to Pratt, educated Pigot's passion, and he ignores the possibility that her own poetry might disclose her feelings more fully than her marginalia. Pratt thus traces her emotions regarding Byron more in Rousseau's nun than in her own writing, and "Rousseau" (Pratt's creation) therefore becomes complicit in the sentimentalizing of her desires and thus complicit in Byron's idealizing acts of conjuring.

One might say that in tracing only the outlines of their subjects (and not their subjects' own lines on themselves), biographers produce silhouettes. Indeed, the only representations we have of Pigot as a girl are the two silhouettes with which Megan Boyes supplies us. A silhouette can be thought of as the profile of a fantasy, or a fantasy in profile: a negative image turned sideways that allows the imagination to fill it in. Here is how Megan Boyes fills in Pigot's silhouette.

The silhouettes of her as a young woman show a profile of great attractiveness with well-formed features, a well-defined chin—but not aggressively so—and, from what can be seen of the figure, it was slender, with a well-rounded bosom, well-suited to the wearing of the rather clinging clothes of the time which did little to conceal the imperfections of their wearers. There is not the slightest doubt that she must have been a most charming person who attracted a number of admirers of the opposite sex. There is only one though who can really be said to have reached her heart and he was a young Army Officer called Hall, possibly from Mansfield and related to her on the Pigot side of the family. He remains rather a shadowy figure but is known to have served in India and died young, with the result that Elizabeth never married.[12]

The silhouette of Pigot itself could not be more well suited to concealing the plainness of its subject; like her departed Hall, she remains "a shadowy figure," which of course makes conjecture easy.

Byron too, so fully represented in portraits, nevertheless found himself treated like a silhouette, encased in the fantasies of both his fans and his biographers. Every silhouette is a double image, both a profile of the person who is drawn and a profile (psychological record) of the person who sees and interprets it. (By making her own silhouette, Annabella Milbanke, as we shall see, produced a representation that, for all its likeness to her, baffled Byron; the story of their facing, fascinating profiles appears in Chapter 3.) Like their subjects, biographers have fallen prey to Byron's spells: they refrain from reporting certain aspects of their subjects precisely in order to supply themselves with materials for a pretty—or prettified—romance. In an important sense, biographers soberly imitate Byron's playful tendency to engage in sentimental idealism.

Byron's dalliance with verse takes on an almost programmatic character in the juvenilia, and it is worth pausing to consider how and why this came to be so. *Fugitive Pieces* (1806), his privately circulated first book of poems, presents an array of occasional pieces, school exercises, and sentimental lyrics but contains little evidence of his promise as a poet. Puerile, sometimes prurient, and always derivative, this collection is largely homage to Thomas Moore (alias Thomas Little), whose songs and poems Byron claimed to know by heart.[13] When he looks into that heart and writes, then, one is not surprised to see the spirit—if not the letter—of the man who would later become his fast friend and first offical biographer. Moore was also an erotic poet, and Byron, a blossoming roué, followed his lead in this vocation as well.

Such a form of imitation, however, spelled trouble for Byron. Many poems in *Fugitive Pieces* strike too close to the homes of the young girls they allude to, and Byron early learned the sting of censure. The Reverend Mr. Becher, to whom Byron sent a copy of his poems, urged him to stop versifying his lovemaking, and in order to redirect the energies of the young poet, Becher himself wrote a poem.

> Say, Byron! why compel me to deplore
> Talents designed for choice poetic lore,

> Deigning to varnish scenes, that shun the day,
> With guilty lustre, and with amorous lay?
> Forbear to taint the Virgin's spotless mind,
> In Power though mighty, be in Mercy kind,
> Bid the chaste Muse diffuse her hallowed light,
> So shall thy Page enkindle pure delight,
> Enhance thy native worth, and proudly twine
> With Britain's Honors, those that are divine.[14]

Becher's advice amounted to an injunction against Byron's playing a Galeotto, a maker of seductive texts. At this point in his career, Byron accepted the criticism; he repossessed as many copies of *Fugitive Pieces* as he could find and burned them—an act that foreshadowed the fate of his memoirs at the hands of his friends.[15]

Yet Becher's stiff criticism did not prevent Byron from continuing to write and rewrite a number of poems that would offend Southwell's inhabitants. He also cut his teeth on Greek translations, one of which obliquely justifies his affinity for an erotic Muse. In "To His Lyre," Byron translates Anacreon's poem as a way of explaining—or having Anacreon explain—why he sings such lusty songs. First publicly circulated in *Hours of Idleness* (1807), Byron's draft of this poem is watermarked 1805. He apparently reworked it for publication, for he wrote to his friend Edward Noel Long on April 16 that his new collection contained "a number of new things . . . among them a complete episode of Nisus & Euryalus from Virgil, some Odes from Anacreon, & several original Odes" (*BLJ* 1:115). Of the nature of his revisions, Byron told Long that "many of the new poems are enlarged and altered, in short you will behold an 'Old friend with a new face'" (*BLJ* 1:115).[16] Here is Byron's translation of Anacreon's Ode 1.

> I wish to tune my quivering lyre,
> To deeds of fame, and notes of fire;
> To echo from its rising swell,
> How heroes fought, and nations fell;
> When Atreus' sons advanc'd to war,
> Or Tyrian Cadmus rov'd afar;

> But still, to martial strains unknown,
> My lyre recurs to love alone.
> Fir'd with the hope of future fame,
> I seek some nobler hero's name;
> The dying chords are strung anew,
> To war, to war, my harp is due;
> With glowing strings, the epic strain,
> To Jove's great son I raise again,
> Alcides, and his glorious deeds,
> Beneath whose arm the Hydra bleeds;
> All, all in vain, my wayward lyre,
> Wakes silver notes of soft desire.
> Adieu ye chiefs, renown'd in arms,
> Adieu the clang of war's alarms.
> To other deeds my soul is strung,
> And sweeter notes shall now be sung;
> My harp shall all its powers reveal,
> To tell the tale my heart must feel,
> Love, love alone, my lyre shall claim,
> In songs of bliss, and sighs of flame. [*CPW*, 1:73]

Byron's repertoire of Anacreon translations includes also Odes 3, 5, 16, 34, and 47, all of which deal with the praise of male and female beauty, the delicious agonies of seduction, or (as in Ode 16) the realities of being a casualty of love: "By Streams of heavenly force I die, / The Lightning of a rolling Eye" (*CPW* 1:10). It would be easy enough to dismiss these translations as school exercises, but they contain the germ of Byron's instinct for fashioning a poetic personality and for creating the self-conscious program of Greek desire that would stay with him throughout his career, a symbolic itinerary that finally landed him in Greece, the locus (classicus) of his erotic—and perhaps existential—imagination.

Byron's selection of Ode 1 in particular allowed him to begin a game of detachment and poetic irresponsibility that would also serve him to the end of his life. His poem to Pigot is a part of this series of feints, flinches, and strategic indirections. In "To His Lyre," Byron deflects attention from his role as an erotic poet by putting the responsibility for his amorous lay-making on the very instrument of poetry. In early Greek poetry, Anacreon's erotic verses signal a shift from a Homeric muse, who celebrates battles, to a post-Homeric muse, who celebrates marriages of the gods.[17] By choosing to translate Anacreon's odes, therefore, Byron determines the nature of his subject matter, and the coercions of Anacreon's lyre seal the case for Byron's lack of will, and hence culpability, in the way he "recurs to love alone."

Byron represents himself as trying to follow Becher's advice to write patriotic poetry, but the lyre's strings simply will not be tuned for transmitting "the epic strain." Perhaps Byron puns on the word "strain" in order to indicate the tension produced by an obligation to write epic verse. He salves his conscience by trying again and again to make the lyre swell with the "glorious deeds" of epic figures, but the lyre will not cooperate. The passive constructions in the poem—especially "are strung anew" and "my soul is strung"—argue for the poet's necessary acquiescence to the material his lyre claims for itself. Following the lyre, Byron makes love, not war, in his poetry—although his literary affairs with women would develop into an erotic agon.

We see here the first pulse of what would become the grand pose in the love life of Byron and of Don Juan, both of whom appear more ravished than ravishing. Curiously enough, the line "I seek some nobler hero's name" anticipates the first line of the mock epic Byron writes to secure his "future fame": "I want a hero"—taking "want" here to mean both desire and lack. Indeed, in choosing Don Juan for his hero, Byron negotiates between the claims of epic and the claims of eros. The sexually put-upon figure of Juan also represents Byron's desire to advertise on a grand scale his own heroic passivity and thus forms an implicit rationalization for his own, often feverish, sexual pursuits. In this early translation, however, Byron contents himself with the excuse that he is being led astray by his "wayward lyre."

The most significant play on words in this poem appears, of course, in the double meaning of "lyre." In a translation of Anacreon the lyre may seem innocent enough, a mere commonplace, but in the context of Byron's early literary "spells" and deceptive enchantments, it takes on new, duplicitous meaning. One might characterize Byron's circumspect, erotically charged poetic experiments as the achievement of a quivering liar, a young man who is learning that "silver notes of soft desire" make for potent seductions.

Despite the critical reception of *Fugitive Pieces*, Byron's unchaste Muse prevailed and allowed him to grow into a master conjurer of the beautiful images he used to seduce his private circle of readers, many of whom came to see the young poet as abusing his power of enchantment. He quickly learned styles of intrigue that sometimes cloaked his intentions but sometimes actually invented the audience for his poetic lovemaking. At the end of the early phase of his life and career, Byron bound his mightiest seductive spells in Cantos 1 and 2 of *Childe Harold's Pilgrimage*, where he most successfully publicized a literary personality that he claimed is not his own. His readers, however, insisted on seeing the Childe's guilty luster as the poet's and thus showed their complicity in the Byron legend. Several women also tried to work their spells on Byron, reforging him from the fantasies he advertised. A number of altogether varnished scenes (of writing) resulted from this interest in returning the favor and the fantasy of Byron's "songs of bliss, and sighs of flame."

If Byron's response to Pigot's quatrain was his earliest—and perhaps most benign—experiment in self-conscious, inverted hypocrisy and sexual idealization, this experiment became a routine in many other poems appearing in *Poems On Various Occasions* and *Hours of Idleness*, and it culminated in *Manfred*. These exercises generated a countermovement in Byron's poetry once he felt himself under the spell of a woman's beauty. His "Stanzas to [Mrs. Musters] on Leaving England" (1809), written just before his trip to the Iberian Peninsula and the Levant, demonstrates Byron's difficulty in breaking away from Mary Chaworth, his first attachment.[18] The penultimate stanza sums up his distraction.

> I've tried another's fetters too,
> With charms perchance as fair to view;

> And I would fain have lov'd as well,
> But some unconquerable spell
> Forbade my bleeding breast to own
> A kindred care for aught but one. [*CPW* 1:268]

By the following January, in Athens, Byron had learned how to use his poetry as a counterspell with which to disenchant himself. His disappointing infatuation with Mrs. Constance Spencer Smith yielded a moment of clarity.

> The spell is broke, the charm is flown!
>   Thus is it with life's fitful fever:
> We madly smile when we should groan;
>   Delirium is our best deceiver.
> Each lucid interval of thought
>   Recalls the woes of Nature's charter,
> And he that acts as wise men ought,
>   But lives, as saints have died, a martyr. [*CPW* 1:280]

Much later Byron would write to John Murray, his publisher, about his lifelong subjection to women: "I have been their martyr. . . . My whole life has been sacrificed to them and by them" (*BLJ* 6:257). Yet he perennially sacrificed women on the altar of his deceptions, and this resulted in a competitive martyrdom or, in my terms, a contest to see who could be more spellbound by the other's literary (mis)representations.

Byron's knack for turning the tables and seeing the Southwell bevy as the greatest purveyors of guile appears most forcibly in "To Woman" (*CPW* 1:45), probably written between 1805 and 1806 as a companion piece to "To Lesbia" ("To Julia" in *Fugitive Pieces*). In this poem, Byron refers to "Woman, that fair and fond deceiver, / How prompt are striplings to believe her" (ll. 11–12). Against the capricious tendencies of women, Byron poses a durable, and commonplace, maxim: "This Record will for ever stand, / 'Woman thy vows, are trac'd in sand'" (ll. 21–22). Woman, for Byron, cannot give her word or, if she does, it cannot last.

Once again Pigot called Byron's bluff. In one of only two extant letters she wrote to Byron, we get her witty reply to "To Woman."

Southwell July 3, 1807

Our cottage is dull without you, and I sit down in my own armchair and wish it were *better filled*—not that I mean to say you are broader than me. Adieu!! Ever believe me though I *am* a *woman*, I have a sincere and affectionate esteem for you. Would it was written in Roberts' Indelible Ink, but tis not in *sand* at all events.[19] [Original emphasis]

Just as Pigot demurred at being the subject of Byron's idealizing lyre, so here she demanded not to be the generalized target of a conventional complaint. That she actually wrote out many of his early poems for him made good her claim that her trustworthiness was not merely a matter of vows marked in sand.

Judging by what Byron confessed to her, Pigot won and indeed earned his full confidence, even the disclosure of the object of his most recent erotic enticements. Byron's letters to Pigot during the summer of 1807 echo those he had written to Augusta three years earlier. They show off his bored profligacy and new amours, and display for Pigot a side of his character few women had seen. She seemed quite able to puzzle through the sometimes recondite grammar of his self-glamorizing confessions. Byron wrote nine letters to Pigot, six of them between June 11 and October 26, 1807, from Cambridge and London. He devoted most of his letters to describing university life, discussing the vicissitudes of his physique, alluding—discreetly—to his liaison with Cambridge chorister John Edleston, and denigrating Southwell. The following passage, taken from his letter of June 30, is typical.

I find I am not only thinner, but taller by an Inch since my last visit, I was obliged to tell every body my *name*, nobody having the least recollection of my *visage*, or person.—Even the Hero [Edleston] of my Cornelian (Who is now sitting *vis a vis*, reading a volume of my *poetics*) passed me in Trinity walks without recognizing me in the least, & was thunderstruck at the alteration, which had taken place in my Countenance &c.&c.—Some say I look *better*, others *worse*, but all agree I am thinner, more I do not require.—I have lost 2 LB in my weight since I left your *cursed, detestable* & *abhorred* abode of *Scandal, antiquated virginity*, & universal *Infamy*, where excepting yourself & John Becher, I care not if the whole Race were consigned to

the *Pit* of *Acheron*, which I would visit in person, rather than con-
taminate my *sandals* with the polluted Dust of *Southwell*. [*BLJ*
1:122–23]

Clearly, the haughty young lord had shaken the prudery of
Southwell from his feet. His concern about staying thin—a
continual worry throughout his life—probably found an added
motive in his desire to imitate his newest idol, the hero of his
poem "The Cornelian," printed in *Fugitive Pieces*.[20]

Byron described Edleston to Pigot in a way that makes it dif-
ficult to tell who is the idol of whom: "You may have heard me
observe he is exactly to an hour, 2 years younger than myself, I
found him grown considerably, & as you will suppose, very
glad to see his former *patron*.—He is nearly my height, very
thin, very fair complexion, dark eyes, & light locks, my opin-
ion of his mind, you already know, I hope I shall never have
reason to change it"(*BLJ* 1:123). Edleston's soul—best repre-
sented through his angelic voice and no less beautiful than his
slender body—Byron clearly adored and envied. A few lines
from "The Cornelian" show the degree of the poet's erotic and
imaginative investment in the Trinity choirboy.

1.
No specious splendour of this stone,
    Endears it to my memory ever,
With lustre only once it shone,
    But blushes modest as the giver.

2.
Some who can sneer at friendship's ties,
    Have for my weakness oft reprov'd me,
Yet still the simple gift I prize,
    For I am sure, the giver lov'd me.

3.
He offered it with down cast look,
    As fearful that I might refuse it,
I told him when the gift I took,
    My only fear should be to lose it.

4.
This pledge attentively I view'd,
    And sparkling as I held it near,
Methought one drop the stone bedew'd,
    And ever since I've lov'd a tear. [*CPW* 1:150]

Byron obviously cherished the cornelian heart Edleston gave him, and this poem symbolically equates the giver and the gift, the stone's dewdrop calling to mind the tears Edleston shed when he offered his patron this love pledge. Byron plays Pygmalion in bringing to life his weeping protégé.

But his identification with Edleston simultaneously reverses their roles, or rather turns Byron into a lachrymose Narcissus, a man who falls in love with the image of his own tears, reflected in the sparkling stone. The cornelian contains both Edleston's and Byron's tears, giving it that luster with which it shone "only once." On several different levels, Edleston is vis-à-vis Byron, and it is not easy to tell the difference between the idol and the idol worshiper.

A week later (July 5) Byron again wrote Pigot and told her of Edleston's departure.

My life here has been one continued routine of Dissipation, out at different places every day, engaged to more dinners &c. &c. than my stay would permit me to fulfill, at this moment I write with a bottle of Claret in my Head, & tears in my eyes, for I have just parted from "my Cornelian" who spent the evening with me; as it was our last Interview, I postponed my engagements to devote the hours of the Sabbath to friendship, Edleston & I have separated for the present, & my mind is a Chaos of hope & Sorrow. [*BLJ* 1:124]

Later in this letter Byron says of Edleston ("my Cornelian"): "I certainly *love* him more than any human being, & neither *time* or Distance have had the least effect on my (in general) changeable Disposition.—In short, We shall put Lady E. Butler, & Miss Ponsonby to the Blush, Pylades & Orestes out of countenance, & want nothing but a Catastrophe like Nisus & Euryalus, to give Jonathon & David the 'go by'" (*BLJ* 1:124–25).

In replying, Pigot, keenly aware of Byron's penchant for making idols of love objects, warns him that his worship of Edleston may have unhappy results: "It delights me to hear you mention your Cornelian in such affectionate terms. . . . Be content to emulate the Moderns in your friendship; the catastrophe of the ancient world would be too much though I do not know anyone more likely than yourself to emulate the 'Fiery Twins.' You have not that name of *Bulldog* for nothing."[21] Even as Pigot shows remarkable insight into Byron's capacity for enjoying male friendships, she explicitly warns him against those that may include sexual relations by calling them a "catastrophe," echoing the word Byron had used to characterize the bond (and the double slaying resulting from it) of Nisus and Euryalus, a story that he had translated from the ninth book of the *Aeneid* and published a few months earlier in *Hours of Idleness*.

Although the translation is little more than a school exercise, some of its details suggest the depth of Byron's passion for friendships modeled on classical stories of what we now call male bonding. Byron is Nisus to Edleston's Euryalus, whose image he polishes.

> No lovelier mien adorn'd the ranks of Troy,
> And beardless bloom yet grac'd the gallant boy;
> As yet a novice in the martial strife,
> 'Twas his, with beauty, valour's gifts to share,
> A soul heroic, as his form was fair;
> These burn with one pure flame of gen'rous love,
> In peace, in war, united still they move;
> Friendship and glory form their joint reward,
> And now combin'd they hold the nightly guard. [*CPW* 1:77]

Much later, in his Ravenna journal, Byron would recollect the purity of his love for Edleston, echoing the language of this passage.[22] Lord Lovelace (Ralph Milbanke) observed that Byron was always seeking literary images of himself.[23] He might have added that Byron was also seeking literary images of those for whom he had conceived great passions, so that others could be translated into the language of his desires. Indeed, in rendering this particular episode from the *Aeneid*, Byron literarily Pygmalionized the model friendship of Nisus and Euryalus in order to enter into a kind of competition not only with Virgil, but with his characters as well.

Byron's braggadocio in his July 5 letter to Pigot, then, consists in upstaging the famous couples to whom he alludes. In a note on the letter, Marchand explains that Lady Eleanor Butler and Sarah Ponsonby, who lived together for fifty years, "dressed as men, but their sexual ambivalence was generally regarded as an amiable eccentricity."[24] Byron's own sexual ambivalence may be registered in the kinds of friendships he chose to mimic.

Playing the game of coded and loaded allusion, Pigot's response claims that Byron is under the third sign of the zodiac: that is, he is an emulator of Castor and Pollux, those "Fiery Twins" in the constellation known as Gemini. Pigot no doubt feared that Byron and Edleston were becoming such twins, fired by their mutual passion. "Bulldog" may simply refer to Byron's tenacity, or bullheadedness, in doing as he pleases.[25] Pigot seems to be recommending that Byron temper his passions and demonstrate some prudence in a friendship that, if literature is any measure, will end in painful separation or death. Yet she facetiously consecrates his emulation of Edleston by seeing their male bond as a configuration of heavenly bodies, and in doing this she participates in Byron's sexual astrology. The way Byron translates the end of the Nisus and Euralyus episode now seems more than conventional.

> Celestial pair! if aught my verse can claim,
> Wafted on Time's broad pinion, yours is fame!
> Ages on ages, shall your fate admire
> No future day, shall see your names expire;
> While stands the Capitol, immortal dome!
> And vanquish'd millions, hail their empress Rome! [*CPW* 1:90]

Despite her cautionary advice, Pigot understood Byron's penchant for being starry-eyed about both male and female companions and his habit of wild idealizing. One might say that Pigot was skilled in the grammar of Byron's glamour and learned to read in his constellated desires the letters that may spell future havoc. Her clever advice that Byron "emulate the Moderns" represents her concern for his public image and the dangers of homoerotic intrigues, but her willingness to participate in his rhetorical obliquity—parrying classical allusions with him—also indicates her delight in translating, and gently rebuffing, the language of his passions.

Biographers have always acknowledged Pigot's role as a sympathetic auditor, but they have not made it clear how deeply Byron confided in her; nor have they acknowledged the fact that she was not one of the fair sex to whom he felt he must condescend. Decoding his "Mary" poems for Long seems trivial next to the encoded candor Byron reserved for Pigot. His bond of loyalty to her was due to the reasonableness she encouraged in him, and also to the fact that, however much she enjoyed addressing some of his erotic lyrics to herself, she did not take the consequences of that particular game any more seriously than he did. She alone saw him as a fat, bashful boy who had now grown into a collegiate Anacreon.

After his first grand tour Byron cast his eye and net wide. In his extremely popular *Childe Harold's Pilgrimage: A Romaunt* (1812) and in his oriental tales (1813–15) he still charmed his readers with the glamour of romance, but he interleaved it with high adventure, political allegory, and world-historical *Weltschmerz*. He took the act he had learned in Southwell on a grand tour and returned to England with a wealth of literary lures and fairytale-like enchantments. The oriental tales offer exotic spectacles and attractively doomed (anti)heroes. Although Byron roundly denied that he was any one of his creatures, this protest merely encouraged his readers to pursue the identification, increasing his notoriety by allowing them to see in his menagerie of infidels and pirates the makings of a Regency villain.[26] Byron was one of the first writers to capitalize on sexual secrecy, for in the Giaour's "nameless spells" (*CPW* 3:66) one can see the poet prefiguring what Foucault believes is characteristic of modern people generally: "not that they consigned sex to a shadow existence, but that they dedicated themselves to speaking of it *ad infinitum*, while exploiting it as *the* secret."[27]

Byron's first exploitation of his life and secrets came with the publication of *Childe Harold's Pilgrimage*. Pigot had not been inclined to do anything but play along with Byron's early enchantments; she could, for example, see the young poet's abuse of his powers when he attempted to paint a deceptively beautiful picture of her. Byron did not try her good faith and responded to her relative disinterestedness by making her an early confidante, an ear for his secret wishes. As his popularity soared and the temptation to promote himself increased, Byron became more and more sought after by those who read his literary spells and began to imagine the young poet a thing to be wished for. These readers accordingly fancied themselves his enchanter. Tantalized by *Childe Harold* and what she had heard of its author, Caroline Lamb one day read the poem no more; she wanted to meet the poet at all costs. Pigot's "negative" in every way, Lamb nevertheless wrote her vow of affection for him by practicing the sincerest and, as it turned out, the most indelible form of flattery.

Lady Caroline Lamb dressed as a page, Thomas Phillips. Trustees of the Chatsworth Settlement. The Courtauld Institute of Art, London.

2

Byron's Miniature Writ Large: Lady Caroline Lamb

Having consumed Cantos 1 and 2 of *Childe Harold's Pilgrimage* (1812) and the gossip about Byron, Lady Caroline Lamb determined to meet the author even if, she declared, "he is as ugly as Aesop."[1] After seeing Byron's notoriously pale face she claimed it would ruin her. Gratified by her overtures, Byron told Lamb she was "the cleverest, most agreeable, absurd, amiable, perplexing, dangerous, fascinating little being that lives now, or ought to have lived 2000 years ago" (*BLJ* 2:116)—but he quickly grew to despise her advances. Byron's first full-fledged fan, Lamb wrote her vow of affection for her poet-lover by practicing the sincerest and the most bedeviling form of flattery. One of her more ingenious antics shows how much she knew about her idol, his secrets, and his anxieties about his reputation and authorial responsibility. Her forays into the life of Byron and his reactions to them demonstrate that idol and fan (model and disciple) sometimes reflect, even invent, each other's desires.

In early January 1813 Lamb forged a letter to herself from Byron in order to obtain his favorite portrait of himself—the Newstead miniature—from John Murray, his publisher. Here is the text of her forgery.

Once more my Dearest Friend let me assure you that I had no hand in the satire you mention so do not take affront about nothing but call where I desired—as to his refusing you the Picture—it is quite ridiculous—only name me or if you like it then but this note & that will suffice—you know my reasons for wishing them not to allow *all* who call the same latitude explain what ever you think necessary to them and take which Picture you think most like but do not forget to return

Facsimile Lady Caroline Lamb's forgery. [1—10]

it the soonest you can—for reasons I explained. My Dearest Friend take care of X#X#X#X#X#X#X#X#X#X#X#X#X#X#X#X#X#X#X#X#X#X#X# X#XX#X#X X#X#X#X#X#

Byron[2]

The string of X#s at the end of this transcript represents a series of overscribblings, almost certainly done by Lamb herself as part of her effort to imitate Byron's epistolary style, for his letters show that he often scratched over his lines. In the process of encroaching upon Byron's epistolary identity, then, she practiced *his* art of obfuscation and self-deletion in order better to represent his hand and thus to fool Murray.[3] Lamb did in fact obtain the miniature of Byron she desired; apparently she simply entered Murray's rooms the next day and made off with it. That everybody except Murray believed that the forgery would have been instrumental in procuring the picture is the center of my interest.

This act of forgery and the theft that followed show Lamb's re- (or con-)scripting of Byron's codes of secrecy and his desire to have complete control over the social rituals, images, tokens, and writings associated with his romantic itinerary in Whig society. Examining Byron's responses to Lamb's machinations can help us to explain his concern about the fashioning and proper advertising of his identity, authority, and originality. In Lamb, Byron found a miniature (of himself) to admire and despise. The correspondence between Byron, Lamb, Lady Melbourne, and John Murray in late 1812 and early 1813 gives notice of Byron's often imperiled lovemaking and fame making. Lamb's transgressions, though traditionally treated as hysteria, can be more accurately understood as a spectral pursuit of her own kind of proto-Byronic, erotic notoriety: an imitation of her ideal man.[4] "She did not know it," observes Margot Strickland, "but she was a captive Celtic woman artist, struggling to free herself from oppressive Anglo-Saxon male domination."[5] In her struggle Lamb taught the fledgling Byron about the dynamics of full and partial disclosure, forgery, and Regency code-breaking: exercises he found not only ravishing but imitable. Her forgery had, to reprise Walter Scott's language, "much of glamour might, / Could make a ladye seem a knight." Indeed, such a transformation was one of Lamb's favorite fantasies of emancipation.

The story of Lamb's theft continues on January 8, 1813, when Byron wrote to Murray:

Dear Sir—You have been imposed upon by a letter forged in my name to obtain the picture left in your possession.—This I know by the confession of the culprit, & she is a woman (& of rank) with whom I have unfortunately been too much connected you will for the present say little about it, but if you have the letter *retain* it—& write to me the particulars. You will also be more cautious in future & not allow anything of mine to pass from your hand without my *seal* as well as signature.—I have not been in town—nor have written to you since I left it—so I presume the forgery was a skilful performance. I shall endeavour to get back the picture by fair means if possible.—

ever yrs
BYRON

P.S. Keep the letter if you have it.—I did not receive your parcel & it is now too late to send it as I shall be in town on the 17th.—The *delinquent* is of one of the first families in this kingdom—but as Dogberry says this "is flat burglary"—Favour me with an answer. [*BLJ* 3:11]

Murray ignored Byron's request but apparently sent him the forgery, to which Byron added and signed a bracketed postscript: "This letter was forged in my name by Caroline L. for the purpose of obtaining a picture from the hands of Mr. M.—January 1813." He jotted this note probably for Lady Melbourne, who was the next recipient of the forgery. Sexuality, representation, transgression, and barter crystallize in Lamb's "flat burglary." Her theft associated her, in Byron's eyes, with Dogberry, and clearly what nettled him as much as the theft was its pedestrianism, for she violated both the economy of sexuality and the system of private circulation that were among the chief diversions of the Regency world he had begun to move in.

Byron was right to fear Lamb's imitative talents: the hand was *mistakably* his, and the elliptical language and loose punctuation show that she deftly parroted even his epistolary quirks. Byron's anxiety about Lamb's amorous hectoring now found a solid referent, a representation which was none other than himself: her forgery had purchased, so Byron believed, a Byron in miniature. In the contest of epistolary maneuvering that the theft occasioned it becomes difficult to distinguish Byron from Lamb: his miniature writ large.

Lamb's erotic harassment kept Byron's quill aquiver with excitement and anxiety during late 1812 and early 1813. Spellbound by the transgressions, particularly the written ones, of which Lamb was capable, he prevailed upon Lady Melbourne to help him quiet her. This wish to silence Lamb also resulted from his fear that her flamboyant actions would similarly inspire other women. He admitted as much when he wrote to Lady Melbourne of his desire to keep Lamb from disturbing the peace he enjoyed with Lady Oxford[6]: "All *our* wishes tend to quiet—& any scene of C[aroline]'s will merely involve others in very unpleasant circumstances without tending at all to reunion—which is now absolutely *impossible* even if I wished it.—Besides, as there will be more *breakings* off than one much precious mischief will ensue if her illustrious example (I mean C[aroline]'s) is to be imitated in all quarters" (*BLJ* 2:239). Byron later mimed Lamb's "precious mischief," following the rhythm of transgression and imitation he wished others to avoid but did not avoid himself.

On January 9, Byron told Lady Melbourne what had happened and prevailed upon her to retrieve the picture.

Dear Ly. M.—C[aroline] by her confession has *forged* a *letter* in my *name* (the hand she imitates to perfection) & thus obtained from Mr. Murray in Albemarle Street the picture for which I had restored her own.— —This fact needs no comment from me—but I wish you could reobtain it for me—otherwise I very much fear an unpleasant exposure will transpire upon this subject.— —She shall have a copy & all her *own* gifts if she will restore it to *you* for the present. —This picture I must have again for several weighty reasons—if not—as she has shown an utter disregard for all *consequences*—I shall follow her exampde.—I am hurried now as we are all going out but will write tomorrow dear Ly. M. [*BLJ* 3:11]

Byron believed Lamb perfectly imitated his hand; the parenthetical sentence contains a mixture of disgust and admiration. For all the furor over Lamb's erotic hijinks, he was oddly flattered by her imitations. As in the Narcissus myth, the original admires the copy. But we must also remember that Lamb and the miniature are symbolically in the position of Echo. The miniature was a mimesis of Byron, and Lamb's forged letter was a graphic "Echo," an Echo that got both a desired object and a response. The play of original and copy becomes so complicated here that René Girard's theory of triangulated desire only imperfectly describes it.[7] Lamb's migrations from one vertex, as an object of Byron's desire, to another vertex, as his rival for the miniature, to the point of being the model herself (forcing Byron into the role of the humiliated disciple), make it nearly impossible to see all the angles. The result is a set of intrigues so complicated and self-conscious that it seems to parody Girard's theory of mimetic desire.[8]

In contrast to Caroline's overexposure of Byron, Lady Melbourne allowed him, at least in this instance, a controlled exposure; she was an ideally sympathetic audience. Byron told her just as much as he wanted known. In prevailing upon her to retrieve his miniature, Byron made her an indispensable part of the circuit of deception and desire. A one-woman agency of letters, Lady Melbourne accommodated Byron by becoming his most trusted confidante and even his procurer and dispenser of women, and he reserved some of his most luminous candor for her.[9] Indeed, he wrote her the next day (January 10) to convey his excitement about being the victim of Lamb's ingenuity.

—This morning I heard from town (inclosed a letter from C[aroline] to the person in A[lbemarle] Street) that it was in person she seized upon the picture.—Why she herself should say that she *forged* my *name* &c. to obtain it—I cannot tell—but by her letter of yesterday (which I shall keep for the present) she expressly avows this in her wild way and *Delphine* language—It is singular that she not only calumniates others but even *herself*, for no earthly purpose. I wrote to you yesterday in a perilous passion about it—& am still very anxious to recover the picture with which she will certainly commit some foolery.— —Murray is in amaze at the whole transaction & writes in a laughable consternation—I presume she got it by flinging his own best bound folios at his head.— [*BLJ* 3:11–12]

Byron's emphases suggest that he was still incredulous at Lamb's temerity (and skill) in forging his name.[10] Calling her avowal of the theft "Delphine" is an allusion to the novel of that name by Madame de Staël. Byron (literally) underlined his impression of Lamb's imitative language: she can, he implies, only copy originals. Indeed, Lamb's *Glenarvon*, soon to be written, would be her version of *Delphine*.[11] Her later novels, moreover, repeated her attempt to recreate the Byronic hero in her own fashion. By implicitly impugning her writing as derivative, Byron calumniated her and the originality of her written commerce with him. Only Lamb, however, could so expertly copy his hand, and in this sense *she* was an original. In the midst of all her antics Byron could still say of her: "I do not at

Lord Byron. Stipple engraving by Meyer after J. Holmes. National Portrait Gallery.

all know how to deal with her, because she is unlike every one else" (*BLJ* 2:222).

Byron's letter of January 10 to Lady Melbourne continues to lament his victimization at the hands of Lamb.

I am sure since the days of the Dove in the Ark no animal has had such a time of it as *I*—no *rest* any where.—As Dogberry says "this is flat burglary"—will you recover my *effigy* if you can—it is very unfair after the restoration of her own—to be *ravished* in this way.—I wanted to scribble to you a long letter—but I am called away again—for which *you* will not be sorry—remember C[aroline] is responsible for any *errata* in my letter of yesterday—for I sent you her *own* statement in fewer words. [*BLJ* 3:12]

Was Byron bragging or complaining? The man who thought of himself as a dove (symbol of peace, passivity, and freedom) would write in the following year, "My heart always alights upon the nearest *perch*" (*BLJ* 4:111). Indeed, he wished to retrieve the Newstead miniature in order to give it to Lady Oxford, his most recent perch. Byron nevertheless gleefully advertised his passivity, as we see later in his masterwork, *Don Juan*. That he had "been more ravished . . . than anybody since the Trojan war" (*BLJ* 6:237) both morally exonerated him and, more important, allowed him to assume the pose of a world-historical *homme fatal*.[12]

Sonia Hofkosh thinks this posturing shows Byron's "putting him[self] in the woman's place," and she connects "such feminizing ravishment . . . to the unauthorized tales that undermine his own title to invention, to authorship."[13] In Girard's terms, Byron may be feeling anxious about being a model-author, particularly since he was not in control of the transmission of his works, and so he represented himself as a sexual victim of his disciples, both those who pirated his works and those who jumped in (as Lamb would do in "A New Canto"; see below) to continue them. Thus he deflected his own anxieties about being victimized in the marketplace onto the more pleasurable circumstance of being sexually victimized by women.[14] But the word "ravished" has other connotations. Byron's trumped-up hostility in response to being taken advantage of suggests a connection with the world of ritual and repression Pope so delightfully mocked in *The Rape Of The Lock*, a world mirrored in the sexual deflections and superficies of Regency society, particularly its capacity to magnify its misdemeanors and the social decor of its smallest rituals. In his emotional response to Lamb's theft, Byron indeed magnified the Newstead miniature to grand proportions.

At the end of his January 10 letter to Lady Melbourne, Byron claimed that "C[aroline] is responsible for any *errata* in my letter of yesterday." In the world of signifying letters, Lamb embodied errata in contrast to Byron's candid "truths." A month earlier he had written to Lady Melbourne of Lamb: "Her letters are as usual full of contradictions & *less* truth (if possible) than ever" (*BLJ* 2:264).[15] Until he regained control of his representations, Byron suffered from the errata of Lamb's wild, "Delphine" ways and was effectively made to subscribe to her, just as he believed she subscribed to the writers before her.

On January 11, 1813, continuing his complaint against the malfeasance of Lamb, Byron wrote to Lady Melbourne: "The *worthy* C[aroline] tells me in her last letter that she has now broken all but the 6th & 9th Commandments & threatens to omit the "Not" in them also unless I submit to her late larceny" (*BLJ* 3:12). Lamb had cheerfully erased most of the decalogue's prohibitions. She knew that Byron, a great breaker of commandments and maker of solid ironies, must be partly seduced by this eccentric posturing. Peter Manning observes that Lamb's antic disposition must also have gratified Byron because "her lack of self-control assured him of his greater competence and reliability."[16] But in this case, her behavior was so skillfully intrusive that Byron seemed truly addled. He certainly wasted little time in reporting the jinx she had put on him.

On January 17, 1813, Byron wrote to his friend John Cam Hobhouse: "Car[oline] L[amb] has been *forging letters* in my name & hath thereby pilfered the best picture of *me* the Newstead Miniature!!!—Murray was imposed upon.—The Devil & Medea, & her Dragons to boot, are possessed of that little maniac" (*BLJ* 3:15). The imputation of madness is a matter of course, nor is it surprising to see Byron playfully satanize Lamb or associate her behavior with that of an enchantress. We cannot know why, a full week after he learned that Lamb purloined the picture in person, Byron should tell Hobhouse that her forgery purchased it. Perhaps it makes the story even more bizarre and entertaining, or maybe Byron cannot get it out of his head that his own hand is not solely his: that he can be *forged*, and possibly reforged, by another. Byron later told Henry Fox that Lamb "has the power of imitating [my] hand to perfection to an alarming perfection and still possesses many of [my] letters which she may alter very easily."[17] We know from his own testimony that Byron hated any kind of competition: "I never risk *rivalry* in anything," he told Lady Melbourne (*BLJ* 2:193). In Lamb, he found a dreaded rival and—what is more—a secret sharer of his preferred (self)images.

Although Lamb could be thought of as springing fully formed from the head of Byron, like Athena (knowledge) from

the head of Zeus (power), she actually rewrote this myth by
stealing Byron's head in miniature, reversing the patriarchal po-
larities. In seizing the picture she recapitated Woman and
ravished Byron, whose frantic response suggests that he had
indeed lost his head. For her, the miniature was a toy/token/
copy which she seized, having lost her purchase on the original.
Like Keats's Isabella, Lamb fetishized the head of her absent
lover.[18] She hoped her forgery (of Byron) would procure another,
miniature Byron, which in turn she could use as barter for the
real Byron's attentions.

By March 14, 1813, the miniature was still in Lamb's pos-
session, and Byron seemed almost resigned to its loss, provided
that she remain silent about the matter: "I did & do want the
picture—but if she will adhere to her present silence—I shall not
tempt her into further scribbling.—You will at least allow I have
gained one point—I shall get away without seeing her at all—no
bad thing for the original whatever may become of the copy"
(*BLJ* 2:26). Possession, in several senses of the word, had
become—under Lamb—at least nine points of the law. More
threatening than her keeping the miniature was the menace of
her "further scribbling." Byron felt he had been forged enough
as it was. Twelve days later, however, responding to Lady Mel-
bourne's admonitions that he was "*fussing* about *trifles*," Byron
wrote: "And now pray let me lay my hands upon the picture im-
mediately. It is too bad in C[aroline] to raise up the Ghosts of my
departed vows against me—She made me sign I know not what
or how many *bonds*—& now like a Jew she exacts usurious
interest for an illegal transaction—Pray promise anything—&
I will promise you anything—copies—originals—what you
please—but let me have the picture forthwith" (*BLJ* 3:31).

We can read in Byron's vehemence Lady Oxford's impatience:
she wanted the Newstead miniature for herself. Having signed
"bonds," however, kept Byron conscripted to Lamb, although the
nature of these bonds is not known. For Byron commitment was
usury and Lamb was a Shylock, holding him to the *letter* of his
bond. Writing to Moore of Francis Hodgson (a Cambridge friend
with conventional views), who had been "inoculated with the dis-

ease of domestic felicity," Byron defined constancy as "that small change of Love, which people exact so rigidly, receive in such counterfeit coin, and repay in baser metal" (*BLJ* 5:131).

Lamb's constant attentions to Byron parodied his own cynical description of the pathology of love. On April 5 he complained to Lady Melbourne of Lamb's falsehoods and her exaggerations about the love tokens he had given to her.

The charm of the ring exists only in her own malignant imagination— every *ring* was *English*—I recollect something of a Comboloio or Turkish rosary of amber beads which I gave to her—to which she attached some absurd mystery—but the rings (among them a *wedding* which she *bestowed* upon *herself* & insisted on my placing it on her finger) were all the manufacture of a Bondstreet Artist who certainly was no conjurer. [*BLJ* 3:35]

Lamb, however, was a conjurer. Like the theft and the forgery, her ring trick was a scandal of self-glamorizing and self-authorization, a ritual that required no witnesses. Byron added: "Nothing but a wish to make her act right in giving up what she ought not to retain would have induced me to submit so long to the *fragments* of her yoke—& hear the clanking of the last links of a chain forever broken" (*BLJ* 3:35). The clanking bonds produced a noise Byron was committed to silencing. Later in this letter, after swearing lifelong hatred for Lamb, Byron wrote: "I beg to be spared from meeting her until we may be chained together in Dante's Inferno." A darkly humorous line, this allusion revealed his deep connection to Lamb: equally sinful, they were two of a kind. Byron was referring to Paolo and Francesca, wrapped in each others' arms, buffeted by the hot winds of their desires.[19] Byron knew he was "wedded" to Lamb but chose not to honor the bond until he met her in Hades.

In another letter to Lady Melbourne, Byron admitted that he was indebted to Lamb and would practice a clownish amortization.

I have a long arrear of mischief to be even with that amiable daughter of Ly. B[essborough]'s—& in the long run I shall pay it off—by instalments.—I consider this as payment the first for the bonfire—a debt too heavy to discharge at once.—After all—if from this hour I were never to hear her name mentioned—at least from herself—I should be too happy to let her off with all her laurels—but if she recommences hostilities—I have no protection against her madness but my own foolery—& I shall avail myself of my cap & bells accordingly. [*BLJ* 3:40]

The bonfire Byron refers to was the operatic auto-da-fé Lamb had staged in Brocket in the late fall of 1812, where she burned her lover in effigy along with copies of his letters.[20] As if reborn from these ashes, Byron gladly rose to the occasion of retribution and mischief. Lamb's antics obliged him to repay her, yet he would allow her to escape from the entire affair "with all her laurels" if she would only behave herself. This sarcasm indicates Byron's belief in her mad talent for mischief but also implies his belief that she cannot hope to compete with Regency society's most celebrated jester—who nevertheless tried to bury himself in either anonymity or obfuscation. His fear of overexposure and misrepresentation, intensified during his affair with Lamb, may have curried his talent for posing and indirection, a talent that would help him make *The Giaour* among the most serpentine, most encoded pieces he ever wrote.[21]

Byron's continuing correspondence with Lady Melbourne indicates how many "*fragments* of [Caroline's] yoke" still link him to her. His letter of April 19 (*BLJ* 3:40), for example, makes some puzzling references to *The Giaour* and to the mysterious beginning of Lamb's forgery.

As for C[aroline] I do not know to what she alludes—the thing in question "the Giaour" was written some time ago & printed when you had it—lately—I have had neither time nor inclination to scribble—far less publish.—I asked Ly. O[xford] if she had seen your satire & she tells me she had neither seen nor heard of it—I wonder that any of these *young* ladies you mention should be attacked & still more that I should be presumed the assailant—the mention of any of their names might preserve me from the charge.—If C[aroline] gets hold of "the Giaour" she will bring it in wilful murder against the author—& if she discovers that the hair was that of her "dearest Aspasia," I question whether Medusa's would not be more agreeable. [*BLJ* 3:40]

Byron is referring to one of the fifteen copies of *The Giaour* that had been printed for private circulation in late March 1813.[22] Apparently, Lamb had gotten wind of it and had written to Lady Melbourne for details.

The satire in Lady Melbourne's possession is not explicitly identified, but we should recall that Lamb's forgery begins with an allusion to a satire ("let me assure you that I had no hand in the satire you mention so do not take affront about nothing"). We can assume that in both instances the work alluded to was "Waltz," which he wrote in October 1812 but circulated (anonymously) only the following spring.[23] Lamb would have been personally offended by the piece because she was an accomplished waltzer. Her forgery thus deftly reiterates Byron's standard response (denial) to the inevitable allegations about his authorship of any anonymous satire. Lamb demonstrated that she knew enough about Byron's life and writing habits to do more than imitate his hand; she could parody his intentions as well, and thus expose his desire not to expose himself.

On April 21, two days after his letter to Lady Melbourne about *The Giaour*, Byron struck a defensive pose for Murray: "I hear that a certain malicious publication on Waltzing is attributed to me.—This report I suppose you will take care to contradict—as the Author I am sure will not like that I should wear his cap & bells" (*BLJ* 3:41). "Waltz" was a transparent attack on the Prince Regent and his passion for popularizing this form of dance.[24] Byron essentially repeated the opening of Lamb's forgery in recommending that Murray claim that he (Byron) "had no hand in the satire." We can now appreciate the full measure of Lamb's ingenuity in concocting the forgery; she used her knowledge of a piece of writing that Murray and a few others would have recognized as Byron's. In having Byron deny his authorship of the satire, she brought Murray a document containing both an allusion to "Waltz" and a typical denial of it which could only belong to its author. Lamb knew not only how to imitate Byron's hand in blotting out lines but also how to imitate him in canceling his own responsibility for his writings.

Lamb may have included her reference to this particular work because she saw herself, as well as the Prince Regent, as an object of the satire. Byron's feelings about waltzing were not merely a matter of social and political scorn for the implicit alliance such a form of dance made with Germany: he was clubfooted. But Lamb decidedly was not, particularly on the dance floor. Of her most infamous scene—at a fashionable dinner party where she wounded herself—Byron wrote to his confidante: "What I did or said to provoke her—I know not—I told her it was better to *waltze*— 'because she danced well—& it would be imputed to *me*—if she did not'—but I see nothing in this to produce cutting & maiming" (*BLJ* 3:72). He did not mention what Lamb later told Thomas Medwin:

He had made me swear never to Waltz. Lady Heathcote said, Come, Lady Caroline, you must begin, & I bitterly answered—oh yes! I am in a merry humour. I did so—but whispered to Lord Byron "I conclude I may waltz *now*" and he answered sarcastically, "with every body in turn—you always did it better than any one. I shall have the pleasure in seeing you."[25]

Byron's social and psychological proximity to Lamb is nicely captured in the choreography of the waltz. His acute self-consciousness made him worry that if she danced poorly, people would assume it was because she had to drag him along.[26] Byron, we remember, never risked rivalry in anything. The waltz not only involved close contact ("Hot from the hands promiscuously applied, / Round the slight waist, or down the glowing side" *CPW* 3:30) but also made possible an exchange of partners, a parallel version of sexual promiscuity, and Byron keenly observed that Lamb enjoyed many dancing companions; he unconvincingly transfigured his marginality into voyeurism. She gave him a sweeping image of the very inconstancy he so energetically practiced. Much earlier he had written to Lady Melbourne: "I mean (entre nous my dear Machiavel) to play off Ly. O[xford] against her, who would have no objection *perchance*, but she dreads her scenes" (*BLJ* 2:233).

Byron clearly had no rival in waltzing from woman to woman. Rather, he was rivaled in dancing with *one* woman in particular. In her role as superior waltzer, with all this implied for Byron, Lamb simultaneously played the model and the object of his desire. This was particularly annoying to Byron, since he could neither follow in her graceful footsteps nor keep pace with her dizzying antics. Reviewing her scene at Lady Heathcote's, Byron wrote Lady Melbourne, "She took hold of my hand as I passed & pressed it against some sharp instrument—& said—'I mean to use this'—I answered—'against me I presume' and passed on"(*BLJ* 3:72). Byron's repartee doubles over in meaning. Against the hand she once imitated, Lamb pressed "some sharp instrument." With pen as with knife, she became a phallic monster for Byron, a woman who was too sharp and penetrating for her sex or his. Byron's invention of Gulnare in *The Corsair*, first as a murderous heroine, then as a "faint and meek" woman (*CPW* 3:533), enacted his fantasy of autonomy, a way of regaining a control in fiction that he did not enjoy in life, at least in his life with Lamb.[27]

Lamb's sexual ingenuity and audacity had in fact presented themselves many months earlier when she sent him a gift of pubic hair, presumably in a locket, bearing the inscription:

> Caroline   Byron—
> next to Thyrsa Dearest
> & most faithful—God bless you
> own love—ricordati di Biondetta
> From your wild Antelope[28]

Perhaps Lamb's envoi is a conscious echo of Dante's *Purgatorio* 5.113: "ricordati di me che son la Pia [do thou remember me, who are La Pia]." Suspected of infidelity, La Pia was killed by her husband; she is among the three sinners who were impenitent up to the last hour.[29] Lamb's self-implicating allusion was as racy as her gift. Offering lockets containing such gifts was customary in Italy, but this practice seems to have been so far in violation of accepted amorous rituals in Regency society that Byron a few months later burned it (along with some of her letters) "for certain reasons" (*BLJ* 2:256). He did privately what Lamb, only days later, would do in grand public style in the conflagration at Brocket.

Lamb may have known that "Thyrsa [*sic*]" was the Cambridge chorister John Edleston, and that she took second place next to him; if so, this suggests that Byron had made known to her his relations with Edleston. She evoked Byron's affections for the lovely Thyrza at the same time that she courted comparison with him and thus tried to wed in Byron's mind two kinds of desire he found irreconcilable: erotic love and friendship. In the same letter that alludes to Lamb's "unintelligible wish" for the Newstead miniature, Byron wrote: "She requires FRIENDSHIP—but you know that with her disposition it is impossible" (*BLJ* 2:246). In assuming her place next to the cherished Edleston, Lamb exploited the possibility that Byron would think of her as of his male friend. We should remember that she enjoyed dressing up as a page in order to smuggle herself into Byron's rooms in London. Like her forgery, her costume allowed her the freedom of a "forged" man: "What transvestites love," Baudrillard observes, "is this game of signs, what excites them is *to seduce the signs themselves*. With them everything is makeup, theatre, and seduction. They appear obsessed, first of all, with play itself; and if their lives appear more sexually endowed than our own, it is because they make sex into a total, gestural, sensual, and ritual game, an exalted but ironic invocation" (original emphasis).[30] This form of invocation confused and gratified Byron's erotico-literary appetites and theatrical rituals, just as Lamb's violation of social mores both repelled and fascinated him.[31]

Indeed, Lamb's attempts to ravish Byron sometimes brought him up short. Along with the "ricordati di Biondetta" (souvenirs from [the] little blonde), for example, she sent a letter asking Byron to return the favor: "I askd you not to send blood but Yet do—because if it means love I like to have it. I cut the hair too

close & bled much more than you need—do not you the same &
pray put not scizzors points near where quei capelli grow—
sooner take it from the arm or wrist—pray be careful—& Byron,
tell me why a few conversations with the Queen Mothers
always change you."[32] She not only wanted a gift of Byron's
pubic hair but wanted him to spill a little blood in the process
and to send that, too. Byron might have responded: "Oh hadst
thou, Cruel! been content to seize / Hairs less in sight, or any
Hairs but these!" (Pope, *The Rape of the Lock*, 4.175–76). Lamb
also turned Lady Bessborough (her mother) and Lady Melbourne
("the Queen Mothers") into those castrating females who put
Byron's will in check. She thus terrorized his confidential life
and at the same time solicited his kind offices by having him
recall his confidences to her: that is, by demonstrating that she
knew how to experiment with codes, manipulate allusions, and
barter images as well as any poet. These talents made her an
original among the women Byron had encountered, and he took
pains to learn how to repay her mischief. Finally, in early April,
he came up with his own forgery.

Shortly before April 7, 1813, Lady Melbourne repossessed
Byron's picture, using a stratagem he had recommended to her.
Byron's early threat that he would be "seized by a fit of repar-
tee" should Lamb continue her antics, now came to fruition in
a rakishly clever, heartless coup de grâce.

My dear Ly. M[elbourn]e—"You have gotten ye picture"!!—now—do
not on any account allow it to be taken out of your hands where it
will remain very much to the refreshment of the original—copies &c.
I leave to your discretion. The *double* hair amuses you—she will never
discover the difference—& of *course you* cannot know it or tell it—it
was a lucky coincidence of colour & shape for my purpose—& may
never happen again—& surely it is a very innocent revenge for some
very scurvy behavior. [*BLJ* 3:36]

To satisfy Lamb's request for a lock of Byron's hair, for which
she promised to restore the Newstead miniature to Lady Mel-
bourne, Byron had strategically raped Lady Oxford's locks and
sent one of them instead. Counterfeit hair perfectly repaid

Lamb her forgery. A more deft repartee would be hard to imagine, except perhaps by someone like Lamb, who had in a sense taught him the art of forgery and thus served as *his* inspiration. It is a brilliant irony that when Lady Oxford had to leave Byron, he wrote of her absence: "To tell you the truth—I feel more *Carolinish* about her than I expected" (*BLJ* 3:69).

Who got the last word? Voluble lovers cannot stay out of each other's margins. About five months after Lamb's forgery she gained entrance to Byron's rooms in the Albany, where she came upon a copy of William Beckford's *Vathek*. She scribbled "Remember me" on the book's flyleaf and departed. Upon returning and discovering the inscription, Byron apparently flew into a rage and wrote beneath it his hate poem to Lamb.

> Remember thee: remember thee!
> Till Lethe quench life's burning stream
> Remorse and shame shall cling to thee
> And haunt thee like a feverish dream.
> Remember thee! Ay, doubt it not,
> Thy husband too shall think of thee,
> By neither shalt thou be forgot,
> Thou *false* to him,[33] thou *fiend* to me! [*CPW* 3:84]

Again, Lamb had turned Byron into an angry sub-scribe, a belated presence who would like only to forget her intrusive caprices. Again, Byron was forced to echo her, following "Remember me" with his irritated "Remember thee" (which he echoes twice himself).

For Byron, Lamb's scribblings made her impossible to forget. Her sexual and textual inventions and interventions represent the baser matter—the counterfeit coin—he wanted to keep out of circulation. If I am correct, Byron's hate poem recognizes the threat Lamb posed for him. Her "Remember me" may have been merely the plaintive plea of a sad and dejected lover, but it is difficult to believe that she did not have Hamlet's ghost in her distracted mind when she penned the words, and at least subconsciously she must have wanted those words to resonate with imperious authority. Byron would have little trouble remembering Lamb, though what disturbed him was not her adulteries but rather her fiendish talent for insinuating herself, often in writing, into his life, forcing him fitfully to copy her scurvy yet ravishing caprices.

Lamb interfered with the felicitous opposition of public and private in her breaking of codes. She collapsed the distinction between public and private by practicing the art of "pubic relations." The Latin stem for both "public" and "pubic" is *pubi*—yielding the term *publicus*. The *Oxford English Dictionary* notes that "the change to *publicus* appears to have taken place under the influence of *pubes*, in the sense 'adult men', 'male population.'"[34] A chronic rescripter, Lamb played on the prurient sense of *pubes* and thereby subjected her favorite adult man to the fierce whims of her pubescence, perfectly literalized in her vending of her private parts.

Byron, for his part, could not keep these delicious indecencies private. He publicized Lamb's *pubes* by telling Lady Melbourne of them, and this was precisely the kind of betrayal Lamb answered in *Glenarvon*. Her private parts were meant for him alone, just as she wished his private part (the miniature) to be hers alone. Like Byron, Lamb feared losing control of her token representations, of being exposed to others for what she was. Of the exposure of Calantha (the lead female character in *Glenarvon* and Lamb's alter ego), Lamb wrote:

Her letters he had shewn; her secrets he had betrayed; to an enemy's bosom he had betrayed the struggles of a guilty heart, tortured with remorse, and yet at that time at least but too true, and faithful to him. 'Twas the letters written in confidence which he shewed! It was the secret thoughts of a soul he had torn from virtue and duty to follow him, that he betrayed![35]

Lamb herself had just reprinted an alleged letter from Byron, thus striking back at his betrayals by imitating his crime. Indeed, all of *Glenarvon* betrayed the secrets of two of the most important houses in London, and therefore her novel offered a scandalous copy of the original erotic intrigues she had helped to create.

For Byron, all these private parts (pictures, letters, lockets) were elements of a vast social and sexual circulatory system, the operation of which he wished to keep mostly secret, leaking only bits and pieces to his confidante as a guarded advertisement of his immense popularity and sexual notoriety. Directly connected to his desire not to expend himself on or with women was his fear of losing control of his self-identity, especially during the early years when he was building and protecting his name. Lamb's ability to slander this name made her more than a flattering echo, and Byron recognized that his Regency society was in fact big enough for two Narcissi. But his reaction to the purloined Newstead miniature merely repeated Lamb's responses to his betrayals and deceits. The hexed dialectic of original and copy articulated both in the forgery and in the Newstead miniature briefly empowered Lamb and put Byron in some compromising and revealing positions.

Lest matters get out of his control, he destroyed the evidence, just as he had earlier destroyed his first volume of poems (*Fugitive Pieces*) after they had been judged indecent. Lamb's *pubes* thus became merely the latest in a series of fugitive pieces, and they suffered the same fate. She also burned a private part of Byron: his letters—though only the copies made by her own hand, the originals being too precious to destroy. The originals reminded her of the stubbornly original man over whom she was increasingly losing control. Her theft of the Newstead miniature desperately reiterated her attraction to Byron, but at this point she had to settle for a diminished currency and gaze in vain upon the reduced image of the man whose most private parts—his letters, his secrets, his body— she had once shared. She had to endure the miniaturizing of her original pursuits. When Lamb finally traded her copy of Byron's image for what she thought was a lock of the original's hair, she was trying to barter her way back into the mainstream of his affections and self-representations. When Byron sent her a lock of Lady Oxford's hair—mocking Lamb's talent for forgery—he gave her counterfeit currency and thus destroyed her bargaining power. Being jilted by Byron meant settling for fainter and fainter reproductions of the original.

Lamb's publication of *Glenarvon* in the spring of 1816 tried once again to subvert Byron's control over his social appearances, though he claimed not to have been touched by her depiction of him.[36] As a roman à clef, it made no claims to originality, but Lamb was trying to be original only in the sense of exploiting the primary material of her life in Regency society. She cared less to gratify public opinion than to flout it, and she did her work with the diligence of a woman creased with bitterness, frustration, and ennui.

For Lamb, the novel was an immolation and a self-immolation. Although she enjoyed the measure of fame the work brought her, many of her Regency peers, and particularly her husband, were dismayed. When she later heard of Byron's quip to Madame de Staël—that Lamb's portrayal of him would have been better had he been willing to sit longer—she burned all her copies of *Glenarvon* and thus tried to give them the value that ritual violence bestows on its objects, some of those objects being the alleged letters from Byron nested in the novel, burning once again. But no one was present to share the scene, or rival it. In this auto-auto-da-fé, Lamb disappeared in the smoky dialectic of forgery and original.

Byron's contempt for women writers was undoubtedly intensified by Lamb's ability to make a scene in writing, and he came to rue the attention his sudden fame invited even as he could not help but be flattered by it. For Byron, Lamb was both the woman who knew too much and the woman who wrote too much. He ironically honored her wish to be remembered in Canto 2 of *Don Juan*.

> Alas! the love of women! it is known
>   To be a lovely and a fearful thing;
> For all of theirs upon that die is thrown,
>   And if 'tis lost, life hath no more to bring
> To them but mockeries of the past alone,
>   And their revenge is as the tiger's spring,
> Deadly, and quick, and crushing; yet, as real
> Torture is theirs, what they inflict they feel.
>
> They are right; for man, to man so oft unjust,
>   Is always so to women; one sole bond

Awaits them, treachery is all their trust;
    Taught to conceal, their bursting hearts despond
Over their idol, till some wealthier lust
    Buys them in marriage—and what rests beyond?
A thankless husband, next a faithless lover,
Then dressing, nursing, praying, and all's over.

Some take a lover, some take drams or prayers,
    Some mind their household, others dissipation,
Some run away, and but exchange their cares,
    Losing the advantage of a virtuous station;
Few changes e'er can better their affairs,
    Theirs being an unnatural situation,
From the dull palace to the dirty hovel:
Some play the devil, and then write a novel. [*CPW* 5:152]

Certainly seeing herself as the target for this last bit of sarcasm, Lamb struck back one more time by demonstrating that she could play Byron's satiric game and, what is more, that she could do it in ottava rima, a thing unprecedented for a woman.[37] As if her whole vocation were endless Byronic imitation, Lamb responded to the publication of *Don Juan* by writing and anonymously publishing "A New Canto" in the summer of 1819. The piece represents her second major forgery of Byron's hand, but this time he was not on or in the scene to jest or joust with her.

Critics and biographers have not studied this work in any detail. In *The Byron Women* (1974), Margot Strickland does not acknowledge the poem as a self-conscious forgery of Byron's work. Citing the opening line ("I'm sick of fame—I'm gorged with it"), she remarks that this is the beginning of "a long, wittily prophetic poem [Lamb] published in 1819," and refers readers to an appendix where "A New Canto" appears without introduction or illustrative notes.[38] Bernard Grebanier damns the forgery in *The Uninhibited Byron* (1970); calling Lamb's poem "a highly ineffectual and confused would-be satire of twenty-seven stanzas," he goes on to complain that "it was absurd of her to think she could in any way diminish or share in his accomplishment with her own anemic verses." He then quotes eight lines from the poem and concludes, "This sally . . . made no impression on anyone."[39] Like many who turn their gaze on Lamb, Grebanier diminishes her accomplishment. The two major biographies of Lamb, Elizabeth Jenkins's *Lady Caroline Lamb* (1932) and Henry Blyth's *Caro: The Fatal Passion* (1972), do not even mention "A New Canto."

In his chapter on the continuations of *Don Juan*, Samuel Chew wastes little time dispatching "A New Canto": "The planlessness of Byron's thirteenth canto is here anticipated; Juan's adventures are postponed to a future installment; and this canto is chiefly concerned with an account of Doomsday and of how it will affect various personages. This theme gives an opportunity for heterogenous satire of a very stupid kind."[40] Chew does not attribute this piece to Lamb, and it is not clear who among her contemporaries detected her hand in the forgery. Although he is right to remark the heterogeneity of "A New Canto," Chew belittles its farrago of styles, moods, and critical observations—Lamb's version of that "wilderness of the most rare conceits" (*CPW* 5:619) which Byron called *Don Juan*.

Far more generous than his predecessors in noting the ingenuity of "A New Canto," Peter Graham argues that in Lamb's impersonation "she implicitly reveals a shrewd and profound understanding of *Don Juan* and Byron alike." Graham wisely observes that Lamb's assumed role as Byronic poet allows her to "at once enjoy the active satisfaction of dealing out vengeance herself and the more passive one of being avenged by the poet she still loved too well."[41] Perhaps Lamb did not love Byron much by this time, but she still enjoyed both miming him and offering some pointed criticism of his poems. Her poetic ventriloquism allowed her to assume the life-size proportions and voice of Byron, but in this forgery she scorned the sentimental and exotic poetry that had seduced not only herself but many others eager to see the young Lord as a fanciful creature: part poet, part pirate.

I content myself here with suggesting the general tenor of the piece and examining in detail some of its richer moments.

Lamb's poetic cameo succeeds not only in sounding, at times, like Byron but also in displaying her own weariness at sounding and acting Byronic. Indeed, the opening stanza mixes these successes.

> I'm sick of fame—I'm gorged with it—so full
> I almost could regret the happier hour
> When northern oracles proclaimed me dull,
> Grieving my Lord should so mistake his power—
> E'en they, who now my consequence would lull,
> And vaunt they hail'd and nurs'd the opening flower,
> Vile cheats! He knew not, impudent Reviewer,
> Clear spring of Helicon from common sewer.[42]

Like a surfeited Childe Harold, Lamb apes Byron's pose of world-weariness and almost makes him regret the day when hostile reviews incited him to take his poetic vocation more seriously.

We must remember that Lamb's infamous reputation resulted in part from her insistence on actively involving herself in the life of her hero, and in this stanza she shows just how much she knows about the history of Byron's rise to fame. The "northern oracles" refer generally to Scottish reviewers, specifically to the powerful *Edinburgh Review*, whose attack on Byron's *Hours of Idleness* (1807) occasioned his first major work, *English Bards and Scotch Reviewers* (1809). After Byron became world famous in 1812, Lamb-as-Byron[43] notes, early reviewers pretended to have detected his genius from the beginning ("they hail'd and nurs'd the opening flower"). Lamb claims that the "impudent Reviewer"[44] could not distinguish the "clear spring" of Byron's early verse from the "common sewer" of truly bad poetry. In fact, Byron's early verse contains little evidence that he would become a poet of consequence, and one is not surprised to learn that few scrambled to hail the blossoming of his career. What we have in this first stanza, then, is Lamb's favorable, if late, review of Byron's early poetry. At the end of "A New Canto" she turns again to the spectacle of Byron's meteoric fame and his poetic oeuvre.

The bulk of "A New Canto" presents Lamb's wish to bury Regency society. She imagines London swallowed up in a "delicious chaos" of earthquake and volcano in which she too will perish; in this wish she echoes "The Triumph of Dulness" at the end of Pope's *Dunciad* (1743):

LO! thy dread Empire, CHAOS is restored;
Light dies before thy uncreating word:
Thy hand, great Anarch! lets the curtain fall;
And Universal Darkness buries All. [4.653–56]

Pope's finale reverses genesis and has apocalyptic proportions. Lamb's doomsday poem is no less ranging than Pope's, but her tone is gleeful. Her chief delight consists in describing how people of all classes and professions will be consumed.

The ball comes tumbling in a lively crash,
And splits the pavement up, and shakes the shops,
Teeth chatter, china dances, spreads the flash,
The omnium falls, the Bank of England stops;
Loyal and radical, discreet and rash,
Each on his knees in tribulation flops;
The Regent raves (Moore chuckling at his pain)
And sends about for Ministers in vain.

And a few stanzas later:

Who would be vain? Fair maids and ugly men
Together rush, the dainty and the shabby,
(No gallantry will soothe ye, ladies, then)
High dames, the wandering beggar and her *babby*,
In motley agony, a desperate train,
Flocking to holy places like the Abbey,
Till the black volumes, closing o'er them scowl,
Muffling for ever, curse, and shriek, and howl. [*NC* 213]

Lamb's urbane malice most resembles Byron's satire when she attacks hack writers and poets. This is a mode Byron first practiced in *English Bards and Scotch Reviewers*, his most Popean satire. Lamb's animadversions make for some of her best poetry.

Save London, none is wickeder, or bigger;
An odious place too, in these modern times,
Small incomes, runaways, and swindlers eager
To fleece and dash; and then their quacks and mimes,

> Their morals lax, and literary rigours,
> Their prim censuras [*sic*], and their gendered rhymes—
> Mine never could abide their statutes critical,
> They'd call them neutral or hermaphroditical. [*NC* 215]

I have seen neither a manuscript copy nor an early edition of "A New Canto," but I suspect that "censuras" (not, to my knowledge, a word) ought to be "caesuras." Perhaps, however, "censuras" is a pun. Like both Pope and the poet in whose voice she spoke, Lamb linked literary corruption to moral chaos. That she was herself a poetic mime makes the stanza buckle with irony, a cramp reproduced when Lamb self-critically refers to her/his rhymes as "hermaphroditical." Critical of anything prim and gendered, Lamb contains the possibility of both male and female rhymes.

Near the end of her poetic impersonation Lamb reverts to her opening theme, Byron's literary career and fame. The following stanza, for example, offers a less than approving review of Byron's exotic verse tales in general, and in particular his tendency to idealize the settings where his fictional lovers mate.

> What joke?—my verses—mine, and all beside,
> Wild, foolish tales of Italy and Spain,
> The gushing shrieks, the bubbling squeaks, the bride
> Of nature, blue-eyed, black-eyed, and her swain.
> Kissing in grottoes, near the moon-lit tide,
> Though to all men of common sense 'tis plain,
> Except for rampart and amphibious brute,
> Such damp and drizzly places would not suit. [*NC* 216]

Here Lamb sounds a little like the "northern oracles" who disliked the young poet idling his hours away with dull, impossibly sentimental verse. In this stanza, however, her attack focuses on the oriental tales and early cantos of *Don Juan*. The "bride of nature" probably refers both to "The Bride of Abydos" (1813) and to Haidee in Canto 2 of *Don Juan* (1819).[45] In both works excitable, dark-eyed women find themselves in wet, cavernous, would-be romantic settings.[46] Lamb's Byronic satire on

Byronic eroticism and exoticism (the oriental tales) also offers a proleptic criticism of yet another grotto love scene in *The Island* (1823).[47] In this stanza Lamb works through her anxiety about the charges of hysteria and obsessiveness which her Regency peers leveled against her by satirizing the seductive fictions that had once made her shriek and bubble over their author. It is convenient that the narrator of *Don Juan* usually debunks romantic sentimentality (with the notable exception of the Haidee episode), for this allows Lamb to assume his voice and mark her distance from the "foolish tales" that first captivated her.

The penultimate stanza of "A New Canto" begins with an apostrophic summation, excoriates contemporary critics, and then winds up for a self-reflexive finale.

> Mad world! for fame we rant, call names and fight—
> I scorn it heartily, yet love to dazzle it,
> Dark intellects by day, as shops by night,
> All with a bright, new speculative gas lit.
> Wars the blue vapour with the oil-fed light,
> Hot sputter Blackwood, Jeffrey, Giffard [*sic*], Hazlitt—
> The Muse runs madder, and, as mine may tell,
> Like a loose comet, mingles Heaven and Hell. [*NC* 216]

In a mad world one simultaneously courts and disdains fame. Lamb spoke for herself and her model author when she offered this sly appraisal of what Leo Braudy calls "the frenzy of renown." In writing "A New Canto" Lamb tried to participate in the repute of her self-exiled former lover, but her failure even to sign the piece indicates the diminishing returns she expected from her literary excursions. Perhaps, like Byron, she assumed that her readers would see through the piece to its author.

In her satiric mode, like Byron, Lamb names names. "Blackwood" is William Blackwood, the bookseller who distributed Murray's books in Scotland.[48] "Giffard" is William Gifford, John Murray's literary adviser and the first editor of the *Quarterly Review*. "Jeffrey" is Francis Jeffrey, editor of the *Edinburgh Review*. "Hazlitt" is William Hazlitt, essayist and lecturer, a man who, Byron wrote in his journal, "talks pimples—a red and white corruption rising up (in little imitation of mountains upon a map), but containing nothing, and discharging nothing, except their own humours" (*BLJ* 8:38). Lamb suggests that these four men compete with—or perhaps sputter their disapprobation of—Byron's dazzling genius and his mad muse. This muse of enchantment is, of course, also Lamb's. As in the first stanza, here Lamb assumes a protective stance toward Byron's achievement, though clearly she enjoys proclaiming him dull and foolish or, rather, presenting the fiction of having Byron critique himself in these terms.

The "loose comet" may have been lassoed from *Manfred*: "A wandering mass of shapeless flame, / A pathless comet, and a curse" (*CPW* 4:57). Like Lamb's Muse, who "mingles Heaven and Hell," Manfred's star, whose "course was free and regular," now hurls itself "Without a sphere, without a course, / A bright deformity on high, / The monster of the upper sky!" A dazzling and dangerous body, Lamb was herself a comet loosed on Regency society, a woman whose need for recognition drove her to make scenes, sometimes in writing. Her textual escapades made her a monster among her upper-class peers, and like Byron (and Manfred) she seemed born under a fateful star. She named her star "Byron"—a brightly deformed muse who inspired her to produce her own marriage of heaven and hell.

Lamb concludes "A New Canto" on a playfully abusive, self-regarding note, a note dear to the narrator of *Don Juan*.

> You shall have more of her another time,
> Since gulled you will be with our flights poetic,
> Our eight, and ten, and twenty feet sublime,
> Our maudlin, hey-down-derrified pathetic.
> For my part, though I'm doomed to write in rhyme,
> To read it would be worse than an emetic—
> But something must be done to cure the spleen,
> And keep my name in capitals, like Kean. [*NC* 216]

Aping the Byronic mode, imitating his hand to perfection, is Lamb's therapy, her forgeries the prescriptions she wrote herself in order keep her own name capitalized. Indeed, her desire to be capitalized (celebrated, writ large) is of a piece with her fetishization of the Newstead miniature. In writing "A New Canto" she symbolically put on the head of Byron she had once filched and imitated his satirical and self-ironic stances. She tried to make capital out of her forgery. But ultimately, social misdemeanors kept her name in the diminished print of gossip columns, for contemporary and most modern readers of "A New Canto" find it unimpressive.

The only thing to "cure the spleen" is the exercise of versifying and the pursuit of fame. This malady reminds us of that other famous spleen scene in English literature, Canto 4 of Pope's *Rape Of the Lock*, a satire which, not incidentally, informs some of the rhythms and imagery of her forgery.[49] Lamb's cave of spleen, I believe, parodies the romantic grottoes whose heroes and heroines had once enchanted her. She once bubbled and gushed with the most infatuated of Byron's fans but lived to exchange that lie for the truth of her skepticism and disenchantment.

Thanks to the high-handed dismissals of biographers and literary critics, Lamb's forgeries have received little attention. Her works have been considered a "common sewer" next to Byron's "clear spring of Helicon." But "A New Canto" shows that she also knew how to flatten the sublime, concoct *Weltschmerz* and fey despair, molest critics, gull readers, poke fun at fame, and do it all in frisky ottava rima. She thus imitated and parodied a Byronic mode that first dizzied and later disgusted her.

One year after "A New Canto" was published, Lamb produced her last forgery in person when she appeared at a masquerade as Don Juan, complete with a troupe of devils.[50] Some write a new canto, and then play the devil. Like her hermaphroditical rhymes, Lamb contained both sexes, a truth she presented in one costume after another.

Anne Isabella, Lady Byron. Watercolor by Mary Ann Knight.
Newstead Abbey, Nottingham Museums.

3

The Divining of Byron:
Annabella Milbanke

The worst woman that ever existed would have made a *man* of very passable reputation. They are all better than us—and their faults, such as they are, must originate with ourselves. . . . By the bye, you are a *bard* also—have you quite given up that pursuit?
> —Lord Byron to Annabella Milbanke

You still leave your own wishes in sublime mystery—to try my powers of Divination?
> —Annabella Milbanke to Lord Byron

At the epicenter of Regency society, Byron's poetry and reputation produced tremors in many who knew him. Annabella Milbanke's bardic pursuits and her powers of divination, for example, contained faults—or rather fault lines—that originated with Byron. Like Lamb, Milbanke knew Childe Harold before she met his author, but unlike Lamb, she wished to reform Byron, to exorcise the gloomy Byronic hero from his creator's soul. To do this she turned her own bardic powers on the poet in order to break his spell and put him under hers. Between 1812 and 1815, increasingly harried both by Lamb's imagination and machinations and the pressures of his immense popularity, Byron began to look on life with the wealthy, pious, and extremely well-educated Miss Milbanke as an opportunity to enjoy peace of mind, if not peace of soul. In the midst of his amorous trials with Lamb, Byron wrote to Lady Melbourne: "Does Annabella *waltz*? It is an odd question, but a very essential point with me" (*BLJ* 2:218). He hoped Lady Melbourne would assure him that Milbanke was no Lamb. His question does not appear at all odd when we consider how Lamb had been waltzing circles around him. For her part, Milbanke saw in Byron a confused, melancholy man who needed her to awaken his inner goodness. By reforming England's greatest sinner she could both rewrite *Clarissa* and reverse the rake's progress toward damnation. This chapter examines how the effort to forge a better Byron encouraged Milbanke to "divine" the poet (in both senses), an effort he underwrote and demolished by devious turns.[1]

The story of Milbanke's attempted reformation of Byron can be divided roughly into three periods. Her "Lines supposed to be Spoken at the Grave of Dermody" (1805) and "The Byromania" (1812) show us, respectively, her attempts at graveyard verse and her rebuke of the sentimental idolatry she associated with Lamb's infatuation with Byron and his alluring poses. In the second phase Milbanke wrote salvational poetry, which includes her "Let my affection be the bond of peace," "On seeing in Castle Low Bran a single Lily in a barren spot under a rock," "What Eye Can Search the Ocean Deep," and "Thyrza to Lord Byron."[2] These verses trafficked in a poetry of emulation, but one that cautiously eschewed a craven Byromania and tried instead to reform Byron by appealing to his own love of ideal and idealizing representations. The separation poetry of the third period shows the disenchantment and cunning of both Byron and Milbanke. An unhappily married couple produce what Byron's editor calls "Bout-rimés from Seaham," a collaborative piece of nonsense poetry laced with derision and duplicity. Milbanke's "Response to——'s Professions of Affection" formed her reply to Byron's notorious "Fare Thee Well!" and suggests that she had given up on reforming him. The culminating text in this agon of image-casting was *Manfred* (1816), Byron's response to the attempt to reform him. His most deceiving and self-deceived representation is a hall of smoke and mirrors in which figures from the past materialize briefly and vanish like fugitive allusions. Milbanke saw herself in this poem, although not in the role Byron had intended for her.

One of Milbanke's earliest compositions, "Lines supposed to be spoken at the Grave of Dermody" (1809), was written when she was seventeen. Thomas Dermody (1775–1802) was a minor poet of the period who died young after a short life of misfortune and dissipation. Of his life, the *Dictionary of National Biography* (5:289) concludes: "Worn out in body with disease and privations, and weakened in intellect, he died in a wretched hovel near Sydenham, Kent, 15 July 1802, and was buried in Lewistown Churchyard, where there is a monument to his memory." Dermody was recorded as having said, "I am vicious because I like it." In 1807 *The Harp of Erin, or the Poetical Works of the Late Thomas Dermody*" appeared in two volumes. Ethel Colburn Mayne, one of Annabella's early biographers, publishes most of Annabella's elegy.

> Degraded genius! o'er the untimely grave
> In which the tumults of thy breast were still'd,
> The rank weeds wave, and every flower that springs
> Withers, or ere it bloom. Thy dwelling here
> Is desolate, and speaks thee as thou wert,
> An outcast from mankind, one whose hard fate
> Indignant virtue should forbid to weep. . . .
> The innate consciousness of greater powers
> Than one in thousand know to estimate
> Will with the frown of restless discontent
> Oft mark his brow who owns them. . . .[3]

Through Lamb (Annabella's cousin by marriage) Byron had received this poem along with other verses, and we know what his first impression was: "I have no desire to be better acquainted with Miss Milbanke; she is too good for a fallen spirit to know, and I should like her better if she were less perfect."[4] On May 2, 1812, Milbanke wrote in her diary: "Went in morning to Lady Caroline Lamb, and undeceived her by a painful acknowledgement. . . . Received Lord Byron's opinion of my verses."[5] Presumably the Dermody poem was among them.

Mayne suggests that these verses might have been written "expressly to please him whose brow was so well acquainted with the frown of restless discontent."[6] But at the time of the poem's composition Milbanke could have been acquainted only with *Hours of Idleness* (1806) and *English Bards and Scotch Reviewers* (1809), for brows in various states of romantic agony would not make their appearance until *Childe Harold's Pilgrimage* (1812): "Strange pangs would flash along Childe Harold's brow" (*CPW* 2:10); "life-abhorring gloom / Wrote on his faded brow curst Cain's unresting doom" (*CPW* 2:39), "Nay, smile not at my sullen brow" (*CPW* 2:39). She had seen neither Byron's marked brow in person, nor his fictional brows marked on paper.

Milbanke's "Lines" oddly foreshadowed the saturnine, Cainite heroes Byron would go on to create not only in the person of the Childe but also in the cursed and exiled figures in his oriental tales and especially in *Manfred.* Offered as an elegy, her verses nevertheless memorialized a certain kind of poet and hero. The "untimely grave" no longer encased a "mute, inglorious Milton" but rather "an outcast from mankind." The woman who became Byron's "moral Clytemnestra" (his term) knew how to conjure an audience or a particular reader—or so her biographer claims. Her poem displayed her ability to manipulate the same Romantic commonplaces so congenial to Byron—and to Childe Harold, his creature and double.

Three years later Milbanke had already learned the importance of achieving some critical distance from her elegiac sentimentality, and she wrote another poem to prove it. Her second important poem, also included in Mayne's *Life,* is "The Byromania" (1812), a satiric piece that lashes out at Byron's cult followers.

> Woman! how truly called "a harmless thing!"
> So meekly smarting with the venom'd sting.
> Forgiving saints!—ye bow before the rod,
> And kiss the ground on which your censor trod. . . .
> Reforming Byron with his magic sway
> Compels all hearts to love him and obey—
> Commands our wounded vanity to sleep,
> Bids us forget the *Truths* that cut so deep,
> Inspires a generous candour to the mind
> That makes us to our friend's oppression kind.
> Amusing Patroness of passing whim

Which calls the *weaker* sex to worship *him*,
See Caro, smiling, sighing, o'er his face
In hopes to imitate each strange grimace
And mar the silliness which looks so fair
By bringing signs of wilder Passion there.
Is Human nature to be cast anew,
And modelled to your Idol's Image true?
Then grant me, Jove, to wear some other shape,
And be an anything—except an Ape!!

A.I.M. 1812[7]

Milbanke ironically anticipated her own reformist tendencies by ridiculing such ambitions in others, even in Byron himself, whom she called "Reforming Byron."[8] Byron's flattery had by this time victimized a number of women, most notably Caroline Lamb. Milbanke called attention to Byron's stinging venom and his censorious rod. The language of pain ("wounded vanity," "the *Truths* that cut so deep") underscored her sense of how Byron had oppressed the weaker sex. The truths of male flattery, disenchantment, and inconstancy were precisely the ones against which Milbanke warned women to be on their guard.

In her disdain for the fawning Lamb, Milbanke would seem to corroborate Harriet Beecher Stowe's claim that she "refused to justify or join in the polluted idolatry which defended [Byron's] vices."[9] Lamb, on the other hand, was both a victim and a carrier of the Byronic disease. After a party, a disgusted Milbanke wrote: "I really thought that Lady Caroline had bit half the company, and communicated the *Nonsense-mania*."[10] She censured Lamb's deeply imitative nature and saw in her behavior only a vampirish idiocy. For Lamb—and, interestingly enough, for Byron—the "Idol's Image true" was best captured in the Newstead miniature, though there was no shortage of ideal representations of Byron circulating during this period. Lamb's mistake was in thinking that her miniature Byron, also represented as the romantic quester of *Childe Harold*, bore a natural and necessary resemblance to the original.

Milbanke's skepticism about Byron's self-representations allowed her to see the importance of *not* being magically drawn into them. She simply did not take him, or his fictions, at face value. Participating in his self-representations—in this poem, a matter of physiognomic posturing—meant giving him the lead, making him the model. Doing so would put the participant in the role of the disciple whose wounded vanity must be salved. Milbanke's moral vigilance inspired her instead to make Byron fit into *her* representations of what an ideal, not an idol, looks like. Lamb, Milbanke suggests, worships the false idol of Byronism, and this makes her a Byromaniac, his feckless ape. Milbanke, by contrast, descended from the Mount Sinai of her moral rectitude with conjugal decalogues seared in her heart. Byron and his legend would not easily bite her.

Not quite a hate poem, "The Byromania" is certainly an astringent piece and shows how clearly Milbanke saw through Byron's deceptiveness. It does not show, however, that she saw through herself. "The Byromania" is beguiled by the thing it scorns. Byron himself seemed to sense this when, about two months before his marriage, he wrote to Lady Melbourne of Annabella's affections: "I have always thought—first that she did not like me at all—& next—that her supposed after liking was *imagination*" (*BLJ* 4:229). Her biographers seem to insist that even a fair measure of her *early* liking was owing to her imagination, an imagination partly nourished by Byron's. Mayne speaks of Milbanke's "dwelling too persistently upon the Byronic Legend."[11] She acquainted herself with this legend by reading Byron's exotic poetry. After having read *The Giaour*, for example, she wrote to her aunt: "The description of Love almost makes *me* in love. . . . I consider his acquaintance so desirable that I would incur the risk of being called a Flirt for the sake of enjoying it."[12] And yet Milbanke clearly voted herself least likely to be seduced by Byromania. When she had the chance to meet Byron, she demurred, and the next day wrote her mother: "I did not seek an introduction to him, for all the women were absurdly courting him, and trying to *deserve* the lash of his Satire. I thought that *inoffensiveness* was the most secure conduct, as I am not desirous of a place in his lays . . . so I made no offering at the shrine of Childe Harold" (original emphasis).[13]

By 1813 Byron's literary spells preceded him. Part man, part shrine, he had become a popular idol. As a result, many were unable to separate the man from the legend, transmitted as a series of images and characterizations that variously depicted him. Byron thus found himself drawn into the traffic of representation and idealization which he had presented in his poems. Remarking the similarities between the villain of *The Italian* and the pirate Lara, Walter Raleigh claimed that "the man Lord Byron tried to be was the invention of Mrs. Radcliffe."[14] And Milbanke, observes Malcolm Elwin, "seems to have developed an attitude to Byron much like the mood in which Catherine Morland became General Tilney's guest at Northanger Abbey; from everything she observed, she deduced some diabolic inference."[15]

Byron's poem "Love and Gold," probably written in the spring of 1813, may have been designed to undeceive Milbanke by making a show of his diabolism. E.H. Coleridge conjectures that it was addressed to her, although—as usual—other candidates come to mind as well.[16] In this poem Byron played a familiar game of secrecy and dissimulation.

> I cannot talk of Love to thee,
>   Though thou are young and free, and fair!
> There is a spell thou dost not see,
>   That bids a genuine love forebear.
>
> And yet that spell invites each youth,
>   For thee to sigh, or seem to sigh;
> Makes falsehood wear the garb of truth,
>   And Truth itself appear a lie.

The most charming seductions are the ones conjured from a bashful candor, the poet concocting a secret love potion from the very elements of his disclosure.

> If ever Doubt a place possest
>   In woman's heart, 'twere wise in thine:
> Admit not Love into thy breast,
>   Doubt others' love, nor trust in mine.

> Perchance 'tis feigned, perchance sincere,
>   But false or true thou couldst not tell;
> So much hast thou from all to fear
>   In that unconquerable spell.

The poet allures by equivocation and blames it all on the "spell" of the women, laid down like an animal's invisible scent that makes "the herd . . . throng around." The penultimate stanza foreshadows Byron's unhappy marriage to Milbanke.

> Each day some tempter's crafty suit
>   Would woo thee to a loveless bed:
> I see thee to the altar's foot
>   A decorated victim led. [*CPW* 3:83]

This poem's overarching equivocation lies in the secret spell, which belongs both to the addressee and to the poet, whose "secret thoughts" also cast an "unconquerable spell" over those who wish to discover Byron's deep feelings and meanings. Unable to forbear offering the gift of her genuine love, Milbanke entered the fray of Byronic image-making, her hopes pinned to a talismanic righteousness that unevenly sustained her.

Milbanke's unpublished poem "On seeing in Castle Low Bran a single Lily in a barren spot under a rock," written in June 1814, interweaves images from Byron's poetry with her religious mission to offer succor to the lonely poet. Under the title appears a line from Byron's *Corsair* (1814), which had been published the previous February: "There grew one flower beneath its rugged brow."

> The heart, how like this flower forlorn—
>   Bereft of kindred love—
> "Alone on earth" in wintry morn,
> It still survives the tempest's scorn,
>   Protected from above!—
>
> Its bruised stem that Friend on High
>   Shall suffer not to break—
> Like Hope extend her Summer sky,

> The drooping mourner's tears to dry,
> And buds of Joy to wake—!—

As the epigraph suggests, she had recently read *The Corsair*,[17] and her title, epigraph, and main imagery derive from the penultimate stanza of Byron's tale:

> His heart was formed for softness—warped to wrong;
> Betrayed too early, and beguiled too long;
> Each feeling pure—as falls the dropping dew
> Within the grot; like that had hardened too;
> Less clear, perchance, its earthly trials passed,
> But sunk, and chilled, and petrified at last.
> Yet tempests wear, and lightning cleaves the rock;
> If such his heart, so shattered it the shock.
> There grew one flower beneath its rugged brow,
> Though dark the shade—it sheltered,—saved till now.
> The thunder came—that bolt hath blasted both,
> The Granite's firmness, and the Lily's growth:
> The gentle plant hath left no leaf to tell
> Its tale, but shrunk and withered where it fell,
> And of its cold protector, blacken round
> But shivered fragments on the barren ground! [*CPW* 3:213]

The lily Milbanke spies "under a rock" (she had written "protected by" and then scratched it out)[18] was the "one flower beneath its rugged brow." The pronoun "its" presumably refers to the Corsair's (Byron's) petrified heart, the one "bereft of kindred love" that nevertheless is "protected from above," presumably by the "rugged brow." Such brows, as we have already noted, were associated with Byron and the cult of accursed antiheroes. Here, however, the imagery is more complex, for Milbanke initially seems to be comparing Byron's heart to a lily that survives "the tempest's scorn" because it is sheltered by a rock or, as the epigraph suggests, by a "rugged brow."

The "bruised stem" of Milbanke's second stanza seems to refer to Byron's "gentle plant [that] hath left no leaf to tell its tale." In Milbanke's poem, the lily survives "the tempest's scorn" because it is "protected from above." In this case, the

"Friend on High" must refer to the rugged, protective brow. But this Friend also refers to Milbanke, who wants spiritually to comfort Byron. Finally, "Friend on High" must at some level refer to a benevolent godhead that will protect the damaged stem,[19] which can in this interpretation refer to Milbanke, Byron, or both of them.

Milbanke's "alone on earth" is also a quotation from the end of Canto 2 of *Childe Harold*. Her use of this text identifies her with the solitary and disconsolate poet/wanderer, although Byron's heart was the one in question. It would seem that Milbanke construed her heart in terms of his.

> What is the worst of woes that wait on age?
> What stamps the wrinkle deeper on the brow?
> To view each lov'd one blotted from life's page,
> And be alone on earth, as I am now.
> Before the Chastener humbly let me bow:
> O'er hearts divided and o'er hopes destroy'd,
> Roll on, vain days! full reckless may ye flow,
> Since Time hath reft whate'er my soul enjoy'd,
> And with the ills of Eld mine earlier years alloy'd.
>
> [*CPW* 2:76]

Annabella's poem, compassionating the Childe's experience of loss, tries to offer consolation in the form of a "Friend on High," a sort of vitalizing cherub who causes "buds of Joy to wake."

During this period (1814) Milbanke wrote another poem blending her spiritual hope with Byron's publicized self-torment.

> Let my affection be the bond of peace
> Which bids thy warfare with remembrance cease.
> Blest solely in the blessings I impart,
> I only ask to heal *thy* wounded heart;
> On the wild Thorn that spreads dark horror there
> To graft the Olive branch, and see it bear—
> Behold the scion from the tree of life
> Expand its blossoms midst a world of strife,
> And hope—*believe*, its fruits will ripely bloom

With the same sun that brightens o'er thy Tomb,
The sun of Glory—day-spring from on high—
To souls "in hope to rise," the seraph of the sky.[20]

Milbanke's campaign to save Byron's soul, to make him over
in her own image, began with this poem. She tried to graft her
virtue onto the "dark horror" she associated with his "wounded
heart." Chiefly through his poetry, Byron had everyone believing
that he regularly fell upon the thorns of life and bled. Milbanke's
lugubrious and histrionic language shows her falling in love with
the remorse-torn Byronic hero *in* Byron. He sometimes encour-
aged this confusion, and his turbid moods sometimes did make
him appear as gloomy as any of his heroes.[21] Milbanke tried to
resist falling in love with these Byronic self-representations—a
weakness she denigrated as idol worship in "The Byromania"—
by being more than a mere ape, more than the weak imitator she
saw in Lamb. She attempted to graft something new onto Byron
and the Byronic hero: the "Olive branch" of her affections. But
in doing so she could not keep from citing Byron's poetry. The
quoted phrase "in hope to rise" seems to answer stanza 83 of
Canto 1 of *Childe Harold*.

Yet to the beauteous form he was not blind,
Though now it mov'd him as it moves the wise;
Not that Philosophy on such a mind
E'er deigns to bend her chastely-awful eyes:
But Passion raves herself to rest, or flies;
And Vice, that digs her own voluptuous tomb,
Had buried long his hopes, no more to rise:
Pleasure's pall'd victim! life-abhorring gloom
Wrote on his faded brow curst Cain's unresting doom.
[*CPW* 2:39]

Such language must have looked like a written invitation for
Dame Philosophy—Milbanke in the robes of her piety—to ma-
terialize in the cell of cursed "Byron" in order to "bend her
chastely-awful eyes" on the brow of the man she must redeem.
Indeed, her poem offers the "day-spring from on high" (like the

"Friend on High") to souls that have not, as the Childe has, succumbed to the sin of despair. Here was a Dermody, alive and famous, who could be spared an early grave.

Her "world of strife" is probably an allusion to Canto 2 of *The Bride of Abydos,* which first appeared in early December 1813.[22] If Milbanke had wished to play Medora to Byron's Corsair, she now usurped the place intended for either Augusta or Lady Frances Wedderburn Webster (one of Byron's more prominent love interests in 1814) and played the role of Zuleika to Byron's Selim.

> Thou, my Zuleika, share and bless my bark—
> The Dove of peace and promise to mine ark!
> Or since that hope denied in worlds of strife—
> Be thou the rainbow to the storms of life! [*CPW* 3:135]

She replaced the rainbow with "the Sun of glory" ("the seraph of the sky"), and "the Dove of peace" with "the Olive branch," but her imagery was mostly borrowed from Byron's poetry, on which she grafted her own intentions. Milbanke made Byron's poetry refer to her personally in order to parlay a self-reference into a bid for his nonfictional affections. Planting herself in Byron's poetry was also her way of avoiding the unhappy suggestion that Zuleika was really Augusta. This was not the last time that Milbanke tried to usurp Augusta's place.

During their courtship Milbanke became more and more beguiled by the idea of reforming Byron and casting her own magic spell over him in the form of a tonic anti-Byromania, first concocted as the famous curriculum vitae she wrote out for her ideal husband. If ever a piece of writing was designed to sober Byron, it was Milbanke's list of demands, which she produced at the bidding of Lady Melbourne. Mayne describes Milbanke's response to Lady Melbourne's request: "Eagerly Annabella addressed herself to the task. It was almost as good as writing a Character—it *was* writing a Character of Miss Milbanke's potential husband." Mayne is the only biographer to reproduce this list. Presumably numbers 1, 2, 4, and 6 (below) are not in quotation marks because they are not direct quotations from Milbanke.

(1) Consistent principles of Duty.

(2) Strong and *generous* feelings.

(3) "Genius is not in my opinion *necessary*, though desirable,*if united* with what I have just mentioned."

(4) Freedom from suspicion and from *habitual* ill-humour.

(5) "An equal tenor of affection towards me, not violent attachment."

(6) Fortune enough to keep her as she had been accustomed to be kept.

(7) "Rank is indifferent to me"—but she thought good connections important.

(8) "I do not regard *beauty*, but am influenced by the *manners of a gentleman*, without which I scarcely think that anyone could attract me."

"And she added, Mayne writes, "'I would not enter into a family where there was a strong tendency to insanity.'"[23]

Lady Melbourne sent this list to Byron, and he seemed as baffled by it as he was by her method of producing her own profile. Of Milbanke's prerequisites, Byron wrote back to Lady Melbourne: "She seems to have been systematically Clarissa Harlowed into an awkward kind of correctness" (*BLJ* 3:108). He, of course, had Lovelaced himself into an equally ungainly kind of licentiousness, a turpitude irresistible to a reformer, particularly when the rake in question was both spectacularly famous and, presumably, tractable.

For all his disdain, Byron was perfectly aware of Milbanke's reformist intentions, and before their marriage he often seemed willing to give her the power to model him as she saw fit. On September 18, 1814, Byron wrote to Lady Melbourne of Milbanke's acceptance of his marriage proposal: "I mean to reform most thoroughly & become 'a good man and true' in all the various senses of these respective & respectable appellations— seriously—I will endeavor to make your niece happy not by 'my deserts' but what I will deserve you may reasonably doubt of her merits you can have none" (*BLJ* 4:175). Eight days later he repeated his intention to Milbanke herself.

I am thankful that the wildness of my imaginations has not prevented me from recovering the path of peace.—What an unmerciful prose have

I sent you—or rather am sending—but pardon me—I will compress in future my language—as I have already my feelings—my plans—my hopes—my affection into love—I could almost say—devotion to you— forgive my weaknesses—love what you can of me & mine—and I will be—I am whatever you please to make me. [*BLJ* 4:184]

Into her hands he commended his fallen spirit. Few prospective wives could hope to receive a more docile, frankly uxorious letter from a prospective husband. Byron's unmerciful "pros- ing" had never been so honestly discursive, so piously un- compressed. Milbanke represented for him the last chance to find the straight and narrow path of reform after a life of weary- ing dissipation. He gave her the power she most desired: the ability to turn him into a new Adam, a replacement for George Eden.[24] After conceding that he was "at least above the paltry reluctance of not submitting to an understanding which I am sure is superior to mine," he went on to endow his creator with attributes: "I am certain that you are wiser than me—more re- flective—more dispassionate—surely more good." Milbanke enjoyed the roles of "first friend, "adviser," and "reprover," and Byron would ask her if he had "done good or ill," trusting that upon her answer "would materially depend my estimation of my conduct" (*BLJ* 4:184). In this exalted mood of self-reform, Byron took in marriage the hand that would remodel him.[25]

The mood did not last long. At Seaham, just before his marriage, he was cynically resigned to Annabella's quiet scru- tinizing of his character. He wrote to Lady Melbourne: "I like them [women] to talk, because then they *think* less. Much cog- itation will not be in my favour. . . . I am studying her, but can't boast of my progress in getting at her disposition. . . . However the die is cast; neither party can recede; the lawyers are here—mine and all—and I presume, the parchment once scribbled, I shall become Lord Annabella" (*BLJ* 4:229). Al- though Byron had cast himself in Milbanke's mold, his sense of humor had not been reformed. The letter to Lady Melbourne in which he promised to "reform most thoroughly & become 'a good man & true' in all the various senses of these respective & respectable appellations" suggests the facetiousness with which he regarded at least one of these appellations: "Lord Annabella." Only one more act of scribbling was needed to seal his fate and make him his wife's man-wife.

In his "Epistle to Augusta" (1816), written during the separation from Milbanke, Byron sourly recalled all those who "came unsought and with me grew, / And made me all which they can make—a Name" (*CPW* 4:39). He remembered with bitterness those who either pilloried or pedestaled him. In her courtship poetry Milbanke attempted to make a name for Byron which would replace the name (and the infamy) he and others had previously made for him. She wanted to rename the creature vended to her by the Byron legend, and Byron wryly acknowledged the nominative stock into which her ambitions locked him. Indeed, Milbanke's quasi-Byronic, morally magisterial poetry suggests that she had all along been trying to be "Lord Annabella" herself, and this patronymic ambiguity generated the anxieties about authority, imitation, and reformation at the heart of their highly literary courtship.

Milbanke wrote another (unpublished) sacralizing poem about Byron's possible salvation whose tone and imagery suggest that it dates from this period.

> What eye can search the ocean deep
>   And view the gems unknown
> O'er which its waters rage or sleep?—
>   The eye of Heaven alone!—
> And if on shore the Tempests sweep
>   Some single pearl have thrown,
> Weep, mortal! for a treasure weep
>   To thee how rarely shown.
> And we may weep to know no more,
>   Of feelings, purest best
> While troubles, like the waves, roll o'er
>   The deeps of Byron's breast—
> It is not on our earthly shore
>   Those brighter gems can rest—
> Though we their buried rays deplore
>   To God they shine confest.— —

Milbanke alone (we learn in the second stanza), who repre-
sented the living incarnation of "the eye of Heaven," saw into
Byron's depths. The poem contains ample clues to Milbanke's
anxiety about the difference between Byron's *image*—associated
with tempests and tumult—and his gemlike, ever redeemable
true self. The oxymoron "buried rays" crystallizes this tension.
The poem seems to be an exercise in public relations, a way of
assuring those who see only the raging waters of Byron's pas-
sions that he had indeed pure feelings.[26] But clearly Milbanke
wrote this poem to herself to reprise her role as Byron's savior,
the only woman in England who could see beyond his stormy
image and Byronic (anti)heroism to the "brighter gems" that
miraculously "shine confest" to God.

The diction and imagery of Milbanke's courtship poems
seem partly borrowed from Byron's *Hebrew Melodies*, the
group of lyrics that he wrote between October 1814 and June
1815 for Isaac Nathan, a Hebrew composer who had asked
Byron to write some songs for him to set to music. Milbanke,
no doubt delighted by Byron's choice of subject matter, pro-
duced several fair copies of these songs, and her own poetry
seems both to mirror and encourage her fiancé's—and then
husband's—"religious poetry." Two of her poems, for example,
echo Byron's canceled verses of the text of Psalm 107: 23–30.

> They that go down upon the Deep
>   Behold the Almighty's wonders
> When oer the [deep] deck the surges sweep
>   And Oceans echo thunders—.[27]

Probably the inspiration for her most impressive attempt to
transfigure Byron's profane image is one of the poems collected
in Byron's *Hebrew Melodies*, "Oh! Snatched Away in Beauty's
Bloom," which Milbanke claims Byron gave her before their
marriage.

> 1.
> Oh! snatched away in beauty's bloom,
> On thee shall press no ponderous tomb;

But on thy turf shall roses rear
  Their leaves, the earliest of the year;
And the wild cypress wave in tender gloom:

2.

And oft by yon gushing stream
  Shall Sorrow lean her drooping head,
And feed deep thought with many a dream,
  And lingering pause and lightly tread;
Fond wretch! as if her step disturb'd the dead!

3.

Away; we know that years are in vain,
  That death nor heeds nor hears distress:
Will this unteach us to complain?
  Or make one mourner weep the less?
And thou—who tell'st me to forget,
  Thy looks are wan, thine eyes are wet. [*CPW* 3:294]

E.H. Coleridge suggests that this poem was part of the Thyrza cycle, and Milbanke's poetic response (in her own "Thyrza" poem; see below) would seem to strengthen this view.

"Thyrza," we must recall, was a feminine code name for John Edleston, a Cambridge chorister who died young and became the subject of a number of Byron's elegies from the years 1806–16, four written before Edleston's death and the rest after. Of his college protégé, Byron wrote to his Southwell confidante, Elizabeth Pigot: "I certainly love him more than any human being, and neither time or Distance have had the least effect on my (in general) changeable Disposition" (*BLJ* 1:24–25). In his Ravenna journal, he recollected his "violent, though *pure*, love and passion" for Edleston and, ever since, most Byron biographers have been content to fasten on Byron's underscoring of the word "pure" in order to write sentimentally— rather than sexually—of his relations with Edleston. This view appears most recently in Jean Hagstrum's "Byron's Songs of Innocence: The Poems To Thyrza," in which he writes that "the friendship with Edleston represented moral nobility and emotions as close as Byron ever came to religious exaltation."[28] Because Byron's contemporaries thought Thyrza was a young girl, they shared

this moral interpretation, and in fact Hagstrum is merely echo-
ing their willingness to think well—and purely—of Byron's
desires. The important exception to this biographical common-
place appears in Louis Crompton's *Byron and Greek Love:
Homophobia in 19th-century England* (1985), which contains a
detailed and frank discussion of Byron's bisexual tendencies. Al-
though Crompton relies on mostly presumptive evidence to
demonstrate these impulses in Byron, the poetic and epistolary
evidence he cites makes a compelling case.

One must keep in mind that Byron showed Milbanke one of
Thyrza's tresses in order to prove her (Thyrza's) existence and af-
fection for him. Whose "forged" hair this was we do not know,
but that Byron was, in this instance, beguiling Milbanke is sug-
gested by one of her own recollections of this prenuptial period.

In the hour of partial tenderness which I have described as passing be-
tween us at Seaham, when he named Thyrza, he said—as in reference
to myself—that to him one of the most convincing reasons for be-
lieving in Eternity was that we never *could* LOVE *enough* in this state
of being—that we could not mingle "soul in soul." This is beautifully
expressed in the Hebrew Melody. He had written it out for me, before
I married—with this comment, made evidently as an experiment upon
my feelings, "*perhaps* I was thinking of you when I wrote that."[29]

If we take Milbanke's account at face value, her language sug-
gests that Byron was using his Thyrza poem to indicate that
only after death could he possibly love enough, in which case
the poem "Oh! snatched away in beauty's bloom" bodes ill for
their future. But since such a reading would also appeal to Mil-
banke's strong otherworldly faith, it comes as no surprise that
she should include the phrase "as in reference to myself."
Byron, indeed, encouraged her to do so.

One can easily imagine Byron experimenting with his own
feelings by experimenting with Milbanke's. During this period
he assumed, as Peter Quennell puts it, "the attitude of a *poseur*
who seemed determined to play Petruchio and the Prince of
Denmark as the same part."[30] He was certainly expert in the art
of referential pluralism, an art he practiced in his juvenilia when

he retitled his poems, mixed up names, and invented the generic "Mary" to signify any number of women. These practices show his offhand, sometimes underhanded, way of presenting the images and names in his poetry. Milbanke benignly practiced the same art in order to maneuver her way into the main current of Byron's representations and preferred images, "Thyrza" being—at this point—preeminent among them.

The representation of "Thyrza" first appeared in a series of lyrics at the end of the first volume of *Childe Harold*, and the poems obviously helped to establish grief as a Romantic idiom, natural and persistent, like Aeolian harps, precipices, pansies, idiot boys, and impossibly perfect women (the redemptive feminine of the poet's impossibly divided psyche). Annabella's peculiar strain of Byromania—her effort to redeem Byron by using terms and images dear to his heart—no doubt received further encouragement from Charles Heath's engraving of Byron sorrowing for the loss of Thyrza at the end of *Childe Harold*.[31]

This engraving invited its viewers to indulge in the luxuries of the *coeur sensible*. In Heath's depiction of a lovelorn, transcendentally distracted Byron, the gleaming moon could not be more excrescent, more suggestive of romance, melancholy, and matters celestial.[32] The cherub weeping on the lyre that Byron's left hand holds is an image both of divine commiseration and probably of Thyrza herself (or himself), whose dulcet tones were altogether angelic. At the feet of the weeping cherub lies a scroll and pen. The eye traces a line from the crescent, the tips of which point to and frame Byron's forlorn countenance, and then follows the moonlight from his illumined face to the lyre, the cherub, and down its fair body to the left leg, and finally to the left foot, which points to the neglected pen and scroll. This picture even offers the implements for recording one's reactions. Such an invitation was part of a typically Byronic art of allusiveness, subterfuge, and engagement. Several women realized this is one of the few forms of engagement Byron actually enjoyed cultivating, and so they replied to his engraved grief.

In a discussion of Byron's amorous difficulties, Leslie Marchand cites a letter from Lady Falkland that indicates the kinds of overtures to which Byron, partly because of his elegiac poetry, was subjected in 1812.

Tell me my Byron—if those mournful, tender effusions of your Heart & mind, to that Thyrza, who you lamented as no more—were not intended to myself, I should not have been rash enough to suppose it, did not the date exactly correspond with a severe illness, under which I was, at that time suffering—and indeed was almost reduced to the state you there so pathetically describe . . . but now my Byron if you really believe I could add to or constitute your happiness, I will most joyfully receive your hand—but remember I must be loved exclusively—your *Heart must* be *all my own*—I fear yours is too susceptible—I trust however in future it will be centered in one object only—I could not my beloved Byron brook a second time to be slighted by my Husband.[33]

Lady Falkland was vaguely beginning to learn, as Lamb had already learned, the difficulty of capturing Byron's heart by finding oneself in his poems. Not having Lamb's penchant (or talent) for forging that hand, Lady Falkland tried unsuccessfully to corner Byron by wresting allusions to herself from his poetry to make him offer, in writing, his hand and his heart. Like Lamb, Lady Falkland tried to find allusions to herself that prove she was written in Byron's heart. Byron was indifferent to Lady Falkland, for he had no romantic interest in her. He did not respond to her solicitous letters but practiced the art of awful silence that both Lamb and Milbanke later practiced on him.

Two stanzas from "To Thyrza" (1811–12) also contribute to our reading of the Heath engraving.

> In vain my lyre would lightly breathe!
>   The smile that sorrow fain would wear
> But mocks the woe that lurks beneath,
>   Like roses o'er a sepulchre.
> Though gay companions o'er the bowl
>   Dispel awhile the sense of ill;

Though pleasure fires the madd'ning soul,
   The heart—the heart is lonely still.

On many a lone and lovely night
   It sooth'd to gaze upon the sky;
For then I deem'd the heav'nly light
   Shone sweetly on thy pensive eye:
And oft I thought of Cynthia's noon
   When sailing o'er the Aegean wave,
"Now Thyrza gazes on that moon—"
   Alas, it gleam'd upon her grave. [*CPW* 1:351]

It is from this moon-soaked grave that Milbanke's voice deliv-
ered its message of salvation in her poem. She became "the
heav'nly light" and "the star that trembled o'er the deep" of
Byron's strenuously advertised sad soul. Crompton is right to
observe that "for most female readers 'To Thyrza' canceled the
misogyny of the poem's opening and revealed a man who
needed only another Thyrza to redeem him."[34]

Lady Falkland was not the only woman to be flattered by the
"Thyrza" poems and the bouquet of possible references they of-
fered to their readers. In her unpublished poem "Thyrza to Lord
Byron," Milbanke improved on Lady Falkland's stratagem by
identifying with the dead, beloved Thyrza. The Thyrza poems
encouraged Milbanke to respond to the poet, to set him on the
straight and narrow path of redemption. This poem presents
the spectacle of Milbanke disguised as the ghost of Thyrza.

Thyrza to Lord Byron
O cease, nor let the willing theme
Of past delight thy breast annoy
Indulge not in the selfish dream
That broods o'er unforgotten joy—

No sympathy my shade can feel
In thoughts to human passion given
 But woulds't thou to my presence steal
Direct thy chasten'd strain to Heaven.

I may not breathe in accents low
The solemn secrets of the dead,

The chilling hour that all must know,
The tale that tongue has never said.

But I can ease that tortur'd mind
Where thrilling doubt & anguish reign,
And teach thee where on Earth to find
A rest from care, a truce from pain.

And oh! if e'er in vanish'd hour
Thy much loved Thyrza's name was dear
If e'er her voice assumed the power
To soothe thy heart, to charm thy ear,

Shrink not to mark her alter'd tone
It is not tinctur'd with despair
Thou wert on Earth her dearest one
And art beyond the grave her care.

She bids thee play a humble part
And bind thy faith to Heaven's decree,
Estrange the passions from thy heart
The dross of poor humanity.

And take, 'tis all she can bestow
The blessing, & the power to bless
Thou'lt find Religion's voice below
The talisman of Happiness——

If Milbanke had known that Thyrza was really a boy, she would have been mortified to the marrow. The irony of the "moral Clytemnestra" writing "Thyrza to Lord Byron" would not have been lost on Byron, though we have no record of his response to this poem. Milbanke's tactical use of Thyrza recalls Lamb's attempt to gain Byron's affection by courting comparison with the Cambridge chorister ("next to Thyrza Dearest & most faithful"). Lamb might have had a clue to the identity of Thyrza, and her dressing as a page to titillate Byron suggests that she knew how to excite his bisexual desires. But Milbanke, although she had suspicions, tried to think well and simply of Byron's desires, and so she chose Thyrza as an emissary of her own morally purifying ambitions. She became the dead Thyrza in order to evoke the possibility of spiritual reform, to direct

"Thyrza to Lord Byron"

Byron's "chasten'd strain to Heaven" by putting the injunction in the mouth of one who had once soothed his heart and charmed his ear. She sought, that is, to tune Byron's Anacreontic lyre so that it would estrange its quivering passions and "find Religion's voice." Milbanke's choice of material could scarcely have been more misguided, though her method of appeal perfectly chimed with Byron's sentimental idealism.

The line "I may not breathe in accents low" recalls the opening line of Byron's "Stanzas for Music." Even though we have no record of when Milbanke first saw this undated and unsigned poem, a copy of it did belong to her, and it seems to underpin her verses in spirit, if not in letter.[35]

I speak not—I trace not—I breathe not thy name,
There is grief in the sound—there were guilt in the fame;
But the tear which now burns on my cheek may impart
The deep thought that dwells in that silence of heart.

Too brief for our passion, too long for our peace,
Were those hours, can their joy or bitterness cease?
We repent—we abjure—we will break from our chain;
We must part—we must fly to—unite it again.

Oh! thine be the gladness and mine be the guilt,
Forgive me adored one—forsake if thou wilt;
But the heart which I bear shall expire undebased,
And man shall not break it—whatever thou may'st.

And stern to the haughty, but humble to thee,
My soul in its bitterest blackness shall be;
And our days seem as swift—and our moments more sweet,
With thee by my side—than the world at our feet.

One sigh of thy sorrow—one look of thy love,
Shall turn me or fix, shall reward or reprove;
And the heartless may wonder at all we resign,
Thy lip shall reply not to them—but to mine. [*CPW* 3:269]

Byron's letter to Lady Melbourne dated April 25, 1814, has strongly suggested to some scholars that Augusta was the subject of these verses: "I don't often bore you with rhyme—but as a wrapper to this note I send you some upon a brunette, which I have shown to no one else. If you think them not much beneath the common places you may give them to any of your album friends" [*BLJ* 4:105]. It may be that this brunette was Augusta, but there is only slender evidence that Byron had begun working on "Stanzas for Music" as early as April 25: his letter to Moore enclosing "an experiment, which has cost me something more than trouble" [*BLJ* 4:114] is dated May 4, so he could be referring to these stanzas in the earlier letter. And if Milbanke was one of Lady Melbourne's "album" friends, then the poem could have found its way into her hands and supplied the inspiration for her "Thyrza to Lord Byron," which in many ways sounds like a response to "I speak not—I trace not—I breathe not thy name."

Even though later, in 1817, she got Augusta to confess that the verses were written to her,[36] it would not be out of character for Milbanke, in the throes of her ambition to reform Byron, to believe that this poem cried out for forgiveness—even *her* forgiveness—for the guilty love it proclaims. She could read it, that is, as responding to the poetry she had already written on the subject of grief-stricken hearts and dark souls. We have already seen that one of her lines echoes the first line of Byron's stanzas. Furthermore, the lines "With thee by my side" and "one look of thy love, / Shall turn me or fix, shall reward or reprove," would have reminded Milbanke of the imagery and trembling emotions of her Seaham poetry and the delightfully tractable courtship letters in which Byron prostrated himself before her.

Milbanke's failure to make Byron over in her semi-sacred image has been recounted from several angles, but few biographers or critics have noted the degree to which she came under the spell of Byromania, or how she fell silently in league with the other cult followers. Her poetry, particularly her "Thyrza" poem, shows how far she would go to lure Byron into *her* representations of ideal love, even as she accommodated herself to his form of elegiac worship. When Thyrza claims that Byron will "find Religion's voice below / The talisman of Happiness," "she" probably refers to Milbanke, who represented "Heaven's decree" on earth.

"Thyrza to Lord Byron" also weirdly echoes Milbanke's early "graveyard" verse, the "Lines supposed to be Spoken at the Grave of Dermody," in which she rendered a sympathetic judgment over "the untimely grave" of a "degraded genius." The Dermody elegy must have flattered Byron because it suggested that Milbanke was "one in a thousand" who knew how to estimate "the frown of restless discontent": that is, himself. In fact, in Dermody she found an early image of the "degraded genius" of Byron, a kind of proto-Byron on whom she could pour out both her sorrow and her solace. In her "Thyrza" poem she spoke from the grave in order to "ease that tortur'd mind / Where thrilling doubt and anguish reign." She thus resurrected Dermody as Byron and disembodied *herself* in order to speak with the authority of the dead. Milbanke's earlier poem seems to contain a buried caution, one that nevertheless appealed to Byron by using the Faustian language so close to his heart. The later poem makes the caution explicit, offering Byron the chance not to pattern his life after the unfortunate Dermody.

For all Milbanke's effort to enfold Byron in her saving images, the campaign failed, and she spent her last few months with him trying to prove that he was, in fact, a maniac. One of Lady Byron's friends, Selina Doyle, offered her a clue to the reason she could not have succeeded with Byron: "As a real wife you were contemned, but when you become again the *beau idéal* of his imagination, between the possession of which and him there is an insuperable barrier, you will be a second Theresa (Thyrza), perhaps supplant her totally."[37] One scholar's account of Byron's deathbed ramblings suggests that Doyle may have had a prophetic soul.[38] She was certainly correct to observe that interceding between Byron and his idealizing imagination was like coming between the dragon and its wrath. Miss Doyle did not, however, see how far Annabella also fell prey to the *beau idéal* of *her* imagination, especially in her fantasy of making herself the perfect mate. If Byron wished only to bring a second Thyrza to life from the marble of his memories, then Milbanke wished to find a suitable replacement for George Eden. "Edleston," strangely enough, forms an acronym for "lost eden," and in reforming Byron through the agency of Thyrza, Milbanke tried to regain Eden, whom she had lost. Of course, Byron alone could have deciphered these unwitting allusions. Certainly he had punned wittingly when on September 30, 1812, he said to Lady Melbourne, "I admire your niece [Annabella], but she is meant for Eden" (*BLJ* 2.222).

Byron was not to be reformed, except by his own hand. The beginning of the end of his marriage to Milbanke appears in the only extant collaborative poem, a piece of doggerel McGann titles "Bout-rimés from Seaham," written, he notes, during the separation proceeding. The emphasized lines are Milbanke's.

> My wife's a vixen spoilt by her Mama
> *Oh how I pity poor hen-pecked Papa.*

The Lord defend us from a Honey Moon
Our cares commence our comforts end so soon.

This morn's the first time of many a happy year—
I could not live so long with you, my dear
O ever in my heart the last and first—
And without doubt—it is the very worst.

If rhymes be omens what a fate is ours—
And bread and butter eagerly devours.
My husband is the greatest goose alive
I feel that I have been a fool to wive.

This weather makes our noses blue
Bell—that but rhymes an epithet for you. [*CPW* 3:282]

The squiblike couplets make mock of the couple that produced them. A blue Lady Byron recalled "making bout-rimés together in the drawing room with that sort of mirth which seeks to jest away bitter truths."[39] The parties no longer trafficked in hopelessly idealized images of each other; they jointly produced a poetry not of salvation but of derogation. When, for example, Milbanke referred to Byron as "the greatest goose alive," she may have been winging a dart at his relations with Augusta, whom he affectionately called "Goose."

But the most deviously encoded lines are "If rhymes be omens what a fate is ours— / *And bread and butter eagerly devours.*" Their rhymes had been omens, but Lady Byron wished *her* poems to be good omens to cancel Byron's mad and bad omens. Now she was hard pressed to find a line that could keep his destiny from veering off course. Their "eidolomachia"—a battle of competing images and representations—finally cannibalized any hopes of domesticity, the "bread and butter" of marriage and a tranquil life at Seaham.

"Bout-rimés" shows Lord and Lady Byron trying to articulate their separation anxieties in rhymes, and producing dissonances both in and between the lines. Milbanke had learned from her husband how to bury personal allusions in poetry. When, for example, she wrote, "The Lord defend us from a Honey Moon," she was probably remembering their honeymoon night, and

Byron's gun-toting, hall-stalking antics—or far worse memories may be creased into her line.[40] The last couplet of their poem cleverly enjambs even as their marriage end-stopped.

Byron's rancor culminated in his notorious love/hate poem "Fare Thee Well!" (privately circulated in 1816, though quickly leaked to the public press), which looks for all the world like a remorse-torn elegy on his ruined marriage. It is not well known that Lady Byron wrote a response to her husband's sulfuric poem; indeed, her "Answer to——'s professions of Affection" has never been published as one of *her* poems.

> In hearts like thine ne'er may I hold a place
> Till I renounce all sense, all shame, all grace—
> That seat, like seats, the bane of freedom's realm
> But dear to those presiding at the helm,
> Is basely purchas'd, not with gold alone,
> Add conscience too, this bargain is your own
> 'Tis thine to offer with corrupting art
> The *rotten borough* of the human heart!—

Ione Young's *Concordance* attributes this poem to Byron because she uses the Cambridge edition of *The Complete Poetical Works of Byron* (1905), edited by Paul Elmer More, and he wrongly attributes the poem to Byron.[41] This misattribution is a tribute to Lady Byron's talent for sounding Byronic, though the poem makes little sense if read as coming from her husband. In fact, hers was a hate poem answering a hate poem, and it represented the end of her desire to heal Byron's wounded heart, a heart she finally recognized as thoroughly rotten. The poem's ruling metaphor is political. Her place in his heart is like a "seat" in parliament whose occupier is elected by a "rotten borough." Rotten boroughs are depopulated districts owned by aristocrats; the seats to which they elect MPs are generally regarded as sinecures. These boroughs therefore are "the bane of freedom's realm," just as Byron had been an evil force in the life of Milbanke. After much agony she came to realize she had no place in his rotten heart.

As a coda to the story of Milbanke's ill-starred attempt at the reformation of Byron, we must examine how they took leave of each other on January 14, 1815, after one year of marriage.

> She [Annabella] went into the room where he and the partner of his sins [Augusta] were sitting together, and said, "Byron, I come to say goodbye," offering, at the same time, her hand. Lord Byron put his hands behind him, retreated to the mantel-piece, and, looking on the two that stood there, with a sarcastic smile said, "When shall we three meet again?" Lady Byron answered, "In heaven, I trust."[42]

Milbanke was nothing if not persistent in her spiritual initiatives, and her deft repartee suggests that she still had not given up on Byron or his sin-stained soul. His quip was, of course, an allusion to the opening of *Macbeth*, whereby he comically turned the three of them into the portentous witches. The hand he refused to Milbanke turned coldly against her in a witch drama he included in the work he wrote the following summer, and in this scene he seems almost to be anticipating the place where the three of them would indeed meet again.[43] For the reference to *Macbeth* actually foreshadowed that cauldron of double-entendre and troublesome allusion which was Byron's reply to Milbanke's rejoinder.

In exile, Byron wrote *Manfred*, a poetic hex sent home to work evil on its addressees. It is a tissue of obfuscations and half-formed references of which the vanishing figure of Astarte is exemplary. Byron conjured her from his own image, just as he created Manfred from the image of his remorse-torn self. But this phantom fingered Augusta back home and showed that even the most beautiful images can ruin real people. Byron loosed Astarte on his English readers and let her idealized image disguise his lethal intentions. On one level she was as generic and spectral as any of the various women named "Mary" represented in Byron's juvenilia, but on another level Astarte was meant for Augusta, and Byron had trained his readers to see through the fictional women to the real one. The hideous progeny of Byron's malice and remorse, this closet drama created havoc among its readers.[44]

In Manfred's fantasy of autonomy, Byron rebuked those who presumed to judge and reform him. Milbanke's response to an early manuscript of this work I shall cite by way of conclusion. By April 18, 1816 Lady Byron claimed to have "read the new Drama in two [*sic*] acts which he is about to publish, *Manfred*, [which is] full of murder & mystery, and supernatural agency, and a desire to perplex the reader, exciting without answering curiosity . . . [and] of no consequence whatever as far as I am concerned, for the only character that can be attributed to me, tho' I doubt if it be intended, is a very fine one."[45] In mid-April Murray and Byron were in the process of exchanging proofs, and the "Incantation," which earlier formed part of Act 3 and was called "Ashtaroth's Song," was out of sequence in the manuscript Byron had sent to Murray. How Lady Byron got an advance text of *Manfred* is difficult to know, unless the cautious Murray sent a copy to Augusta to gauge her reaction, and Augusta, being by this time under the protective brow of Lady Byron, handed it over to her. Perhaps Milbanke wondered if Byron was once again making an experiment on her feelings in creating Astarte, of whom a hysterical Manfred confesses: "I loved her, and destroy'd her!" (*CPW* 4:74). But the "very fine" character she attributed to herself was none other than the one Byron intended for Augusta in order to intimate their incestuous past.

Even at a distance, then, through the agency of images and allusions, Byron continued to bedevil the women in his life. Mario Praz justly observes that "Byron felt a perverse joy at the simultaneous presence of the two women [Milbanke and Augusta], with all the amusement and innuendoes and double meanings which it afforded him, and the continual sensation of hanging over the edge of an abyss."[46] In self-exile, Byron continued to indulge himself in this amusement by sending home poems containing scandalous multiple allusions. From Switzerland, he pitted his ex-wife and his half-sister against each other.

Milbanke cautiously imagined that Astarte was the only character that could be attributed to her, and this explains her relative equanimity about a work that would eventually prove minatory to both herself and Augusta. Her interpretation paradoxically idealized Byron as the penitent, remorse-torn husband, the perfect counterpart to the ideal and idealizing wife he had loved and destroyed. From the labyrinth of his character and perplexing (mis)representations, she found a way to his heart through her own. She answered the curiosity he so mischievously excited by imagining—for the last time—the best of him, his new poem, and her possible place in it. Considering the trouble *Manfred* made for her, this last attempt to think well of herself and her exiled husband is as deeply ironic as her earlier attempt to save his soul by speaking to him in the voice of his dead male lover.

Milbanke, who never remarried, spent the rest of her life pursuing a course of anti-Byromania long after Byron was dead. Like Dermody, Byron would go to an "untimely grave" in 1824. That Milbanke was no "forgiving saint"—the term she used to disparage meek followers of Byron—may be seen in the vigilance with which she tried to reform Augusta, both after Byron had permanently left England and after his death. But Augusta thwarted Milbanke's powers of divination by refusing to speak, trace, or breathe the name of her half-brother.

Milbanke's campaign of anti-Byromania would come to fruition a decade after her death when her great apologist, Harriet Beecher Stowe, wrote *Lady Byron Vindicated* (1870), a work that hurled Byron into a lake of fire and canonized his wife. Stowe's defense succeeded in doing for Milbanke precisely what she had tried to do for her husband. Another curator of the Byron legend showed, however, that the poet could in fact be spiritualized if one waited long enough.

Countess Teresa Guiccioli. Engraving by H.T. Ryall after a
drawing by H. Brockedon from Finden's *Illustrations to the
Life and Works of Lord Byron*, vol. 2.

4

Unwriting His Body: Teresa Guiccioli's Transubstantiation of Byron

In order to be truly loved by Lord Byron, it was requisite for a woman to live in an illusive environment for him, to appear an immaterial being, not subject to vulgar corporeal necessities. Thence arose his antipathy (considered so singular) to see any woman he loved eat. In short, spiritual and manly in his habits, he was equally so with his person.

—Teresa Guiccioli

Whether Byron's disgust with the "corporeal necessities" of women reached a Swiftian pitch is a matter of conjecture, but the opinion of Teresa Guiccioli, his Italian lover from 1819 until his departure for Greece in 1824, must be properly weighed. For Jonathan Swift, a woman's processes of elimination produced a crippling.trauma in those unlucky enough to witness them. In "Cassinus and Peter" (1731), for example, two Cambridge undergraduates fall in love, but Cassinus has the misfortune to realize something human, all too human, about his inamorata: "Nor wonder how I lost my Wits; / Oh! Caelia, Caelia, Caelia sh——." A long tradition of disgust and fear regarding the bodies of women reaches an oddly comic climax in these lines, as Swift opposes higher functions (wit, intelligence) to their degrading counterpart.

For Byron, ingestion rather than elimination underlined the animality of women. Responding to Miss Mercer Elphinstone's observation that Lady Caroline and she were putting on weight, Byron wrote: "But why will she grow fat? and you too?

that additional wing (with a bit of breast superadded I dare say)
is worse than waltzing.—But as I actually dined yesterday
myself, I must bear these trespasses" (*BLJ* 2:186). In the letter
that asked Lady Melbourne if Milbanke waltzed, he also com-
plained of his seductive prowess: "I am sadly out of practice
lately, except for a few sighs to a Gentlewoman at supper who
was too much occupied with ye. *fourth* wing of her *second*
chicken to mind anything that was not material" (*BLJ* 2:219;
original emphasis).

Byron wrote Lady Melbourne about Milbanke's dining habits
as well: "I only wish she did not swallow so much supper, chicken
wings—sweetbreads,—custards—peaches & *Port* wine—a woman
should never be seen eating or drinking, unless it be *lobster sallad*
& *Champagne*, the only truly feminine & becoming viands.—I re-
collect imploring one Lady not to eat more than a fowl at a sitting
without effect; & have never yet made a single proselyte to Py-
thagoras" (*BLJ* 2:208). Of Byron's anxiety about his wife's healthy
appetite, Bernard Blackstone writes: "While this may have some-
thing to do with his own horror of obesity and recollections of his
mother's gormandising, there were probably moments at which
Byron saw himself as an homunculus between the steady munch,
munch of Annabella's upper and lower jaws."[1] Camille Paglia
drives the point home: "Byron courts femininity but flees female-
ness. His fear of fat is his fear of engorgement by mother and
wife."[2]

Teresa Guiccioli did not seem to believe that Byron's reac-
tion to the appetites of women ("considered so singular")
contained anything particularly misogynistic. On the contrary,
in his antipathy toward seeing any woman he loved eat she de-
tected a principle consistent with his own asceticism. Guic-
cioli's spiritualized Byron could not brook appetite either in
himself or in women. This rationalization of Byron's "antipa-
thy" suggests to what lengths Guiccioli went to think well, and
spiritually, of her past lover's uncharitable attitudes about her
own sex. Her generous interpretation of Byron's need to make
women live an "illusive environment" preserved her own illu-
sions about him.

During her life with Byron, Guiccioli combined the electric sexuality and literary imagination of Caroline Lamb with the moral earnestness of Annabella Milbanke. It was a blend Byron found so attractive that he agreed to become Guiccioli's *cavalier servente*—a sanctioned male concubine. Her role in Byron's literary life involved copying out his poetry and encouraging his treatment of certain subjects over others. It also involved fashioning the poet's legend with an eye both to his reputation and to her own. In her hagiographical *Lord Byron jugé par les témoins de sa vie* (1868), her bowdlerizings of his writings served to dematerialize the poet and his poetry. If Annabella failed to convert Byron during their courtship and marriage, Guiccioli finally managed to transform him long after his death in the sanctuary of her memories and fantasies. Not content with a pared-down Byronic text, she finally established contact with the spirit of her beloved poet. In doing so, she forged one of the Byron legend's most occult textual fantasies.

Guiccioli's offices as Byron's amanuensis and muse, his poems to her, and his letters home present a comedy of eros—a farce of vying illusions in which Byron and Guiccioli struggle to come to terms with the other's representations. After examining their literary lovemaking, this chapter explores Guiccioli's biography of Byron—a work that transfigures its subject on several levels—and, finally, discusses the available evidence of Guiccioli's séances. In a trance she would communicate with the dead and produce volumes of automatic writing, one of which represents her transactions with Byron's spirit, emancipated from its corporeal necessities and bound to Guiccioli's spell.

By all accounts Guiccioli received an exemplary education at the convent of Santa Chiara. But she seemed temperamentally ill suited to cloistral life, for Byron twice referred in his letters to her dissatisfaction. After promising to make her financially independent, he wrote: "But you are made angry by the mere idea—and want to be independent on your own and to write 'Cantate' in lengthy epistles in the style of Santa Chiara—the convent where you were said to be always in a rage" (*BLJ* 7:152).[3]

Iris Origo notes that Guiccioli tried to change *rabbiosa* (in a rage) into *studiosa* (studious), one of many instances of her cosmetic euphemisms. She partly eased her rage at being walled in by consciously modeling her life after the stories she read or by measuring her present life against those stories. Guiccioli's letters apparently bore the impress of her fascinated bovarysm. For just as Byron once ridiculed Caroline Lamb's "wild, Delphine way of writing," he now chided Guiccioli for imitating the style of Madame de Staël's Italian novel *Corinne*. In a letter to Augusta, Byron characterized his new love interest: "But the Guiccioli was romantic—and had read "Corinna"—in short she was a kind of Italian Caroline Lamb—but very pretty and gentle—at least to me—for I never knew so docile a nature as far as we lived together" (*BLJ* 6:248).

Like Lamb, Guiccioli learned a language of passion from novels, and Byron, once so mired in his own Wertherism, could not resist poking fun at the mimetic sentimentalism of others, particularly when it came to their writing. Yet he continued to bait Guiccioli with works designed to play on her literary nerves. After giving her a copy of Lamb's *Glenarvon*, he wrote to her: "Your little head is heated now by that damned novel— the author of which has been—in every country and at all times—my evil Genius" (*BLJ* 7:37).

De Staël's novel particularly set the lovers at odds. In early March 1820 he closed a letter to Guiccioli with a little jab: "I have read the 'few lines' of your note with all due attention— they are written with your usual eloquence, which you will never lose, until you lose—not a Heart, but Corinne."[4] (*BLJ* 7:38) On the index page of Guiccioli's copy of *Corinne*, Byron had earlier written a letter in English so that others would not understand it, but he included the Italian phrase *Amor mio*, a maneuver hardly designed either to baffle outsiders or to dim Guiccioli's fascination with the novel. Iris Origo observes that several passages of the novel are marked in the same ink as the letter, and quotes one of them: "I had learned to love from the poets, but real life is not like that. There is in the realities of existence something arid, which every effort is vain to alter."[5]

In the throes of her literary love affair with Byron, Guiccioli could not accede to this sterilizing observation. She was, after all, learning love from (and making love to) a poet in "real life," and Byron, half unwittingly, was doing his best to confuse her perceptions. At the bottom of page 92 in her *Corinne*, for example, a note appeared, also in Byron's handwriting: "I knew Madame de Staël well—better than she knew Italy, but I little thought that, one day, I should think with her thoughts."[6] Again, this statement is not likely to subdue Guiccioli's tendency to identify with her favorite novel, but Byron did not at first seem to realize how energetically she modeled her life after the works she read, particularly if the work came to her with Byron's recommendation: "I send you a little book, Adolphe—written by [Benjamin Constant,] an old friend of de Staël—about whom I heard de Staël say horrible things at Coppet in 1816, with regard to his feelings and his behavior to her.—But the book is well-written and only too true."[7]

After luring Guiccioli into this work, Byron then offered his sarcastic review of it: "The true picture of the misery unhallowed liaisons produce is in the Adolphe of Benjamin Constant. I told Madame de Staël that there was more morale [*sic*] in that book than in all she ever wrote, and that it ought to be given to every young woman who had read Corinne, as an antidote."[8] Origo cites this critical remark as an example of Byron's often heartless egoism, his persistent inability to keep from wounding his friends—less out of malice than from ignorance of the effects he was capable of producing. Such an egoism would explain his genuine perplexity at the furor the early cantos of *Don Juan* aroused in England. Byron seemed surprisingly obtuse when it came to the consequences of his own writings.[9]

Byron's antidote poisoned Guiccioli. Two days later, she wrote: "Adolphe! Byron—how much this book has hurt me!"[10] But Byron tossed off her injury: "The circumstances of Adolphe are very different. Ellenore was not married, she was many years older than Adolphe—she was not amiable—etc. etc.— Don't think any more about things so dissimilar in every way" (*BLJ* 7:163). He responded to Guiccioli's interpretation the same

way he responded to Murray and all those who read the open-
ing cantos of *Don Juan* as a straightforward, hateful roman à
clef. Byron offered with one hand what he took away with the
other.

Byron's irritation with Guiccioli's habit of mixing literary
memory and desire also appeared in his reaction to her reading
of *The Lament Of Tasso* (1817). Having read it, she demanded
to know "the secret of the suffering which produced this poem,
and who was the original of Eleonora."[11] Eager only to exploit,
and never to disclose his literary secrets, Byron had little pa-
tience with Guiccioli's prying: "If you know what love is—
if you love me—if you feel—how can you at this moment—
seeing the state of things in which we find ourselves—think or
speak of imaginary things? Have we not only too much re-
ality?" (*BLJ* 6:158). By combing his texts for possible allusions
to their love life, Guiccioli challenged Byron's complacency
about his representations and forced him to confront the re-
sults of his imagination.

The most striking example of Byron's ferocious attachment
to Guiccioli occurs when he suspects her of flirting. The result
is one of the most inflamed jealousy poems ever written.

> [To Teresa Guiccioli]
> I saw thee smile upon another;
> If not a lover or a brother—
> Or both (thus to unite in both
> A Lover's best and worst in guiltiest growth)—
> He had no business there to be—
> Thy smile to him were snakes to me.
> I saw thee smile—deny it not—
> For I was rooted to the spot;
> Nailed to my cross—I bled—and saw—
> And suffered—but could not withdraw. [*CPW* 4:240]

The poem goes on like this for another twenty lines, Byron con-
tinuing to mingle self-pity, rage, and even—oddly enough—
forgiveness. Never happy with rivalry of any sort, Byron demon-

strated how even a wayward smile crucified him. His letters expanded his hurt feelings: "I was right then: what is that man doing every evening for so long beside you in your box? . . . I have noticed that every time I turn my head towards the stage you turned your eyes to look at that man."[12] Guiccioli could not have been more delighted with her lover's outbursts. She wrote on this letter: "Billet de jalousie magnifique—passionné—sublime mais très injuste. Il ne me connaissait encore que depuis trop peu!!!"[13] She had discovered that the way to Byron's heart was through another man's. But she did not finger these delicate nerves, and her constancy prevented Byron from having to bleed on the cross of his covetousness.

An outpouring of Byron's more sober love occurred when he was first separated from Guiccioli, connected only by the symbolic current of his affection. In "To the Po (June 2, 1819)," Byron reworks the myth of Narcissus to include his enamored, far-flung Echo. But his conceit, like his image and tears in the stream, keeps drifting away from him. The poem reveals both the surge of Byronic "reflection" and the force of circumstances that dissipate it.

> River! that rollest by the antient walls
>   Where dwells the Lady of my Love, when she
> Walks by thy brink and there perchance recalls
>   A faint and fleeting memory of me,
> What if thy deep and ample stream should be
>   A mirror of my heart, where she may read
> The thousand thoughts I now betray to thee
>   Wild as thy wave and headlong as thy speed?
> [*CPW* 4:210]

This fetishized river was an image text in which Guiccioli could read Byron's thoughts and fantasize about what those thoughts might be, gazing at his stream of words as he gazes at the Po. Guiccioli enjoyed seeing everything Byron wrote as a mirror of his heart, and so she found in this poem the very image of her own fantasies.

The intensity and deflection of Byron's desire (the poem is addressed to the Po, not to Guiccioli) is pure Petrarch, and this too would have gratified her and given back to her the self-image of Laura. Indeed, Petrarch's fetishizing of the places where Laura once appeared seems to have been on Byron's mind, particularly in this passage:

> The current I behold will sweep beneath
>   Her palace walls, and murmur at her feet,
> Her eyes will look on thee, when she shall breathe
>   The twilight air unchained from Summer's heat.
> She will look on thee,—I have looked on thee
>   Full of that thought, and from this moment ne'er
> Thy water could I name, hear named, or see
>   Without the inseparable sigh for her.
> Her bright eyes will be imaged in thy Stream—
>   Yes, they will meet the wave I gaze on now,
> But mine can not even witness in a dream
>   That happy wave repass me in its flow. [*CPW* 4:211]

In Canzone 125 of Petrarch's "Rime Sparse," the desolate poet found himself in similar circumstances and presented his torment in the language of desire that Guiccioli knew so well and that Byron was quickly learning.

> Ovunque gli occhi volgo
> trovo un dolce sereno
> pensado: "Qui percosse il vago lume."

(Wherever I turn my eyes, I find a sweet brightness, thinking: "Here fell the bright light of her eyes.")[14]

Like Petrarch, Byron could not be fed because the wave of his passion does not flow back to him ("The wave that bears my tear returns no more / Will She return by whom that wave shall sweep?"). Such disappointment is integral to the structure of the *Canzoniere* and allows Petrarch to write another 241 poems. Byron's turgid emotions ("Are not thy waters sweeping, dark, and strong, / Such as my feelings were and are" *CPW* 4:210) make the Petrarchan rhetoric swell with actual rather than poetic desire. In the following lines Guiccioli would have read one thought among the thousand:

> A stranger loves a lady of the land,
>> Born far beyond the Mountains, but his blood
> Is all meridian, as if never fanned
>> By the bleak wind that chills the Polar flood.

Unlike the Po, Byron's blood ran through the artery of a constant desire, one that did not subside or sink away.[15]

The same man who demonstrated such intensity of feeling for Guiccioli also knew how to make her appear, in another context, no more important than a common whore. Byron's letters about Guiccioli to his male companions parodied the displays of affection he offered her. About two weeks after the opera box incident, for example, he wrote to Hobhouse: "You would like the forest—it reaches from here to Rimini.—I have been here these two months—and hitherto all hath gone on well—with the usual exception of some "Gelosie" which are the fault of the climate and of the conjunction of two such capricious people as the Guiccioli and the Inglese" (*BLJ* 6:188). Making fun of his feelings, Byron later in this letter wrote: "I have had the G[uiccoli] (whom I came for) in any case—and what more I can get I know not—but will try—it is much better for beauty than Lombardy" (*BLJ* 6:189–90). These are hardly the words of a man who had committed himself to a woman whom Lady Blessington called his "last attachment." But his poems and letters to her during their Ravenna courtship led her to believe otherwise.

The tangled pleasures of love and image-making reached a consummation in Byron and Teresa's interest in Canto 5 of Dante's *Inferno*. Byron had first made use of the story of Paolo and Francesca in the opening epigraphs to *The Corsair*, all of which he took from that canto. In a letter dated May 3, 1819, his interest reawakened. The literary images associated with the sites of Rimini reminded him of his absent beloved.

I shall seek you, you alone; if only I can see you for a few moments every day, I shall be able to spend the rest of the time with your image;

if there were to be a minute in which I did not think of you, I would consider myself unfaithful. Our love and my thoughts will be my sole companions, books and horses my only distractions, except for a little trip to Rimini, in order not to break a promise made to a friend in England three years ago that, if ever I should see that city, I would send him any tradition about the story of Francesca (if any such remain there) besides what is to be found in Dante. This story of a fatal love, which has always interested me, interests me doubly, since Ravenna holds my heart. [*BLJ* 6:122]

A little over a month later (mid-June of 1819) Byron and Guiccioli read about Paolo and Francesca in her copy of the *Inferno.* "Teresa asked him whether it had ever been translated into English. 'Non tradotto, ma tradito [not translated, but betrayed],' he replies—and thereupon promised her to try his hand at a better rendering."[16] *Francesco of Rimini* (1820) was the result. But their lives were already translating the poem. Their desires had been conscripted (and prescripted) by it; the poet had only to transcribe the intersection of Dante's poetic version and their lived version of the story of Paolo and Francesca. By an odd turn of events, this story, which concerns the fate of lovers swept away by the romantic tale they read, would become a text at the heart of another, often dangerous love affair.

One might call this drama "layered procurement": the story of Paolo and Francesca was to Byron and Teresa as the chivalric stories of Lancelot were to Paolo and Francesca. Dante's couple also suffered from literary forepleasure, moving from text to sex without punctuation. Dante had a remorseful Francesca say: "A Galeotto was the book and he that wrote it."[17] Byron's translation, for reasons beyond my understanding, avoided this word: he rendered "Galeotto fu il libro e chi lo scrisse" as "Accurst the book and he who wrote it were" (*CPW* 4:285). Byron himself was a Galeotto who created seductive images that procured women for him, and Byromania was a testimony to the success of his poetic pandering.[18] For her part, Teresa was happy to inspire Byron's poetry, particularly when it involved great works of Italian literature, but she shrank from the intimation that she was another Francesca, because she did not consider herself an adulteress—although Byron clearly did.[19]

Byron also enjoyed playing the role of a Galeotto in his correspondence with Teresa. At the height of their Venice intrigues his letters cite great literary precedents that pedigree their affair and suggest that he has an afterlife on his mind, in Heaven or in Hell.

> You talk of tears and of our unhappiness; my sorrow is within; I do not weep. You have fastened on your arm a likeness that does not deserve so highly; but yours is in my heart, it has become a part of my soul; and were there another life after this one you would be mine—without you where would Paradise be? Rather than Heaven without you, I should prefer the Inferno of that Great Man buried in your city, so long as you were with me, as Francesca was with her lover. [*BLJ* 6:112]

Apparently Guiccioli wore a small picture (the Italian is *un'immagine*)—probably a miniature—of Byron on her arm. Byron, not to be outdone in these conventional expressions of love, tattooed his heart. We will see to what advantage Guiccioli later reworked this conceit.

Byron usually encouraged Guiccioli to embellish their love affair with literary works, just as he had much earlier encouraged his English readers to see him as a poet who regularly propagated literary images of himself (although he publicly disowned this identification).[20] Like his English readers, Guiccioli could also be quickly disenchanted if she believed a literary work misrepresented him—that is, represented his ill-natured, unromantic, and ironic side. She found, the early cantos of *Don Juan* thoroughly immoral, for example, and—also like her English counterparts—she hugely disliked the "Poems on his Domestic Circumstances." In a letter dated October 13, 1820, she wrote to Byron that she found Don Juan "truly scandalous—they are perfectly right to say that in Donna Inez you have presumed to depict your wife. . . . If I were she, I would have forgiven all your failings of 1816, but I would never forgive those of 1818."[21] And Byron's hate poems, which belied the tearstained page of his "Farewell" verses, bewildered Guiccioli,

who refused either to hunt down his ironies or allow him any
distance on his writings.

Guiccioli clearly did not enjoy the levity and even reckless-
ness with which Byron cast his spells over her and others, but
during their love affair she could do little to subdue the thing
she most feared about him—his sense of humor. Byron simply
could not check his mirth at being pressed into the role of Guic-
cioli's "supernumerary slave."[22] After he died, she finally got the
chance to attach herself to him on her own terms, refashioning
his public image, his poetry, his life, and even his afterlife.

Guiccioli's biography of Byron is a series of recollections
purporting to do two things: judge the man, not the author, and
fill in all the gaps in his life left by previous biographers. In the
introduction to her work, she wrote: "If much has been said of
Lord Byron, has his truly noble character been fairly brought to
light? Has he not, on the contrary, been judged rather as the
author than the man, and have not the imaginary creations of
his powerful mind been too much identified with reality?"[23]
Guiccioli promised "to dispel the shadows which fancy has
raised around his name." In short, she promised to write not a
Byromaniac's biography of Byron but rather one that would
"reveal him in his true light."[24]

How far Guiccioli avoided complicity in "the imaginary
creations of his powerful mind" is precisely the question. For
she often altered these creations in order to make them her
own, citing just those lines of Byron's poetry that helped her
paint the picture she wanted. These exercises showed her predi-
lection for erasing his bawdiness or facetiousness, the better to
demonstrate his antimaterial nature and the deep sentiment
and spirituality always at work in his poetry. The result of her
interventions is a series of half-formed, strategically truncated
images. For those who wish to set the record straight about
Byron, Guiccioli's portrait of the poet will appear grossly dis-
torted.[25] For those who believe, as I do, that representations of
Byron's life and legend always involve one kind of distortion or
another, Guiccioli's depiction of Byron appears as one more in a
series of fantasies about the poet, fantasies he first excited by

advertising his broken and bleeding heart in *Childe Harold's Pilgrimage*, that literary first cause of Byromania.

In the introduction to Part 1 of her *Recollections*, we find telling anticipations of the technique of selective citation Guiccioli often practiced later in her work. After declaring that "Byron's portrait could be better drawn from passages of 'Don Juan,' than from any of his other poems," she went on to cite some stanzas from Canto 15.[26] After quoting all of stanza 12, in which Juan's qualities are favorably contrasted to those of a dandy, Guiccioli trimmed the following stanza (in this and in the following citations the material she quoted is italicized, and the lines she deleted are restored).

> They are wrong—that's not the way to set about it;
> As, if they told the truth, could well be shown.
> But right or wrong, *Don Juan was without it;*
> *In fact, his manner was his own alone:*
> *Sincere he was*—at least you could not doubt it,
> In listening merely to his voice's tone.
> The Devil hath not in all his quiver's choice
> An arrow for the heart like a sweet voice. [*CPW* 5:592]

We must picture Guiccioli in her old age with the complete text before her, mentally erasing what she wanted and needed to forget about Byron's poetry. Here, she bracketed her own doubts about Juan's (and Byron's) sincerity by excising anything that began to qualify what she wanted to believe. No doubt recalling—as so many did—Byron's surpassingly "sweet voice," she also muted the devilishly seductive voice at the end of the stanza.

Her pruning of stanza 16 was even more suggestive of her later attempts to transform Byron's self-allusions.[27] After quoting all of stanza 15, which concludes that Juan had no need to "struggle for priority, / He neither brook'd nor claim'd superiority," Guiccioli included only the first two lines of the next stanza.

> *That is, with men: with women he was what*
> *They pleased to make or take him for; and their*

> Imagination's quite enough for that:
>   So that the outline's tolerably fair,
> They fill the canvass up—and "verbum sat."
>   If once their phantasies be brought to bear
> Upon an object, whether sad or playful,
> They can transfigure brighter than a Raphael. [*CPW* 5:593]

Both Guiccioli's brother and Byron tirelessly reminded her of her "diseased imagination,"[28] and this stanza makes another gibe at women and their fantasies. Guiccioli eliminated the last lines of this stanza, despite the fact that they do little more than expand the criticism already suggested by: "with women he was what / They pleased to make or take him for." It is odd that she called attention to these opening lines, for they would seem to indict, however playfully, the very activity of transfiguration in which she was involved.

Guiccioli completed Byron's poetic "self-portrait" with a citation from Canto 10 in which the narrator is trying to describe Juan's affection for the little Leila. Guiccioli cited only the last part of stanza 54 and not all of that.

> And still less was it sensual; for besides
>   That he was not an ancient debauchee,
> (Who like sour fruit, to stir their veins' salt tides,
>   As Acids rouse a dormant Alkali)
> Although ('twill happen as our planet guides)
>   His youth was not the chastest that might be,
> *There was the purest platonism at bottom*
> *Of all his feelings*—only he forgot 'em. [*CPW* 5:453]

Guiccioli's version of Juan's feelings for Leila supported her insistence that her own relations with Byron were mostly platonic. She here wished to see Juan as Byron and herself as one of his fictional characters. That her own feelings, as reflected in these extremely chaste trimmings from *Don Juan*, were at bottom "the purest platonism" suggests the intensity of her will to spiritualize Byron. If he lightly forgot his platonism, she did not.

Guiccioli's expurgations bring to mind Byron's complaints to John Murray about the editorial treatment of Canto 2 of *Don Juan*. Writing from Venice on April 3, 1819, for example, after recommending that Murray publish the first two cantos together, Byron insisted angrily that there "be no mutilations in either, nor omissions, except such as I have already indicated in letters to which I have had no answer" (*BLJ* 6:104). Three days later he again wrote to his publisher with more explicit directions:

Dear Sir—The Second Canto of Don Juan was sent on Saturday. . . . But I will permit no curtailment. . . . —You sha'n't make Canticles of my Cantos. The poem will please if it is lively—if it is stupid it will fail—but I will have none your damned cutting & slashing.—If you please you may publish *anonymously* [,] it will perhaps be better;—but I will battle my way against them all—like a Porcupine. [*BLJ* 6:105]

The language of mutilation, cutting, and slashing would seem to indicate Byron's textual castration fears, as though the poem, its hero, and the author all risked gelding at Murray's prudent, pruning hands. Indeed, Byron wrote that same day to his friend John Cam Hobhouse: "I have sent my second Canto—but I will have no gelding" (*BLJ* 6:107).

Byron's letters to Murray during the publication of *Don Juan* are filled with anxiety about Murray's bowdlerizings and show the poet's anger at reports of the relentless, canting disapprobation heaped on the early cantos of his mock-epic. Byron flatly refused to flatter his detractors by curtailing his works to improve his image back in England. He went on to lash out at the audience to which he would no longer cater.

Neither will I make "Ladies books." . . . I have written from the fullness of my mind, from passion—from impulse—from many motives—but not for their "sweet voices." I know the precise worth of popular applause—for few Scribblers have had more of it—and if I chose to swerve into their paths—I could retain or resume it—or increase it—but I neither love ye—nor fear ye, and though I buy with ye, and sell with ye, and talk with ye—I will neither eat with ye—drink

with ye, nor pray with ye.— They made me without my search a spe-
cies of popular Idol—they—without reason or judgement beyond the
caprice of their Good pleasure—threw down the Image from it's [*sic*]
pedestal—it was not broken with the fall—and they would it seems
again replace it—but they shall not. [*BLJ* 6:106]

Bravado, insecurity, and spite here vie for supremacy. Byron's
defiance in this letter underscored his desire to be treated on and
in his own terms, poetic and otherwise, and in self-righteously
choosing not to be put back on a pedestal, he asserted his inde-
pendence from Murray's—and England's—will.

In her biography of Byron, Guiccioli resurrected the idol. Her
talent for erasing the letter of Byron's poetry in order to put her
reader under the spell of his spirit appears most conspicuously
in the last chapter of the first part of her *Recollections*, aptly
titled "Qualities and Virtues of Soul" and subtitled "Antimate-
rialism." In this chapter, Guiccioli's Catholicism transub-
stantiated Byron and created out of the body of his texts a host of
holy images. In her gleanings from *Don Juan*, she did what Byron
faulted Murray for doing: she made canticles of his cantos.
Unlike Murray, of course, Guiccioli was trying to produce not an
edition of his poem but rather a portrait of the poet, one that
would finally "reveal him in his true light" by illuminating only
his best parts. Byron no longer survived to prevent his curators
from treating either his poetic images or his public image any
way they saw fit. Such is the fate of any popular idol.

Guiccioli's art of selective citation in this chapter began in a
section celebrating all the lovely women Byron created in his
fiction. After adding long sections of his poetry to her portraits
of Medora, Zuleika, and Adah, she turned to "those charming
children of Nature, Haidee and Dudu,"²⁹ and continued her
work.

> A kind of sleepy Venus seem'd Dudu,
>   Yet very fit to "murder sleep" in those
> Who gazed upon her cheek's transcendent hue,
>   Her Attic forehead and her Phidian nose.
> Few angles were there in her form 'tis true,

> Thinner she might have been and yet scarce lose;
> Yet, after all, 'twould puzzle to say where
> It would not spoil some separate charm *to pare.*
> [*CPW* 5:311; final emphasis Byron's]

Guiccioli clipped the last half of the stanza, for the moment the portrait was anything but completely charming, she pared away, unpuzzled about what parts needed to go. For her, the stanza, like the drowsy Dudu, might have been thinner.

Continuing her catalogue of Byron's fictional women, Guiccioli cited only the first two lines of stanza 46 in Canto 15, and in this instance what she left out struck her where she lived and worshiped. The narrator is describing the prim and silent Aurora Raby.

> *She was a Catholic, too, sincere, austere*
>   *As far as her own gentle heart allowed.* [,]
> And deem'd that fallen worship far more dear
>   Perhaps because 'twas fallen: her sires were proud
> Of deeds and days when they had fill'd the ear
>   Of nations, and had never bent or bow'd
> To novel power; and as she was the last,
> She held their old faith and old feelings fast. [*CPW* 5:602]

But Byron ended his second line with a comma, not a period, so that he could comment on that faith to which Guiccioli had sworn unqualified allegiance. Although Byron may have drawn this woman from his memories of Annabella, his portrait of a sentimental pagan who keeps the fallen faith also calls to mind Guiccioli herself, who here so expertly deleted Byron's casual impiety.

Guiccioli's biographical practices also call to mind Byron's lighthearted reaction to bowdlerizing in Canto 1 of *Don Juan.*

> Juan was taught from out the best edition,
>   Expurgated by learned men, who place,
> Judiciously, from out the schoolboy's vision,
>   The grosser parts; but fearful to deface
> Too much their modest bard by this omission,

And pitying sore his mutilated case,
They only add them all in an appendix,
Which saves, in fact, the trouble of an index. [*CPW* 1:22]

Guiccioli and Murray edited "the grosser parts" of the poem, for both feared that their immodest bard misrepresented—or defaced—himself. Just as Donna Inez wanted Juan to be "taught from out the best edition," so Byron's editor and his Italian lover wished their readers to see his works only in their chastened, mutilated form. Guiccioli expurgated the ironically detached parts of *Don Juan* in order to make herself, indeed, Byron's last attachment. But Byron's delight in deflation, his nearly reflexive bathos, threatened to sink her fantasies.

The twenty-five chapters that make up the published *Recollections* show that Guiccioli's will to apotheosize Byron brooked no obstacle. Her two-volume, 900-page testimony presented a slow-moving and relentless defense of a man whose life had been torn apart by scandal and whose later poetry had given great offense. A glance at the chapter headings reveals the immense range of Guiccioli's reconstruction. In the first volume are chapters on Byron's religious opinions, his friendships, the qualities of his heart, his benevolence and kindness, and, finally, his soulfulness (a chapter whose spiritual agenda I presently examine). The second volume offers chapters on Byron's faults, although Guiccioli excused them all, and others titled, for example, "Lord Byron's Constancy," "Virtues of His Soul," "His Generosity Elevated into Heroism," and finally "Conscience [as] the Chief Quality of His Soul."

Guiccioli's editing of offensive or unsentimental passages from *Don Juan* made her a procurer of (self-)seductive, sentimental images. She became herself a purveyor of romantic illusions, a Galeotto. It is no accident that she asked Byron to stop writing *Don Juan*—or so he told his friends in England. His letter to Murray of July 6, 1821, suggests that he knew why his poem was causing such a stir. "The reason for this is not at first obvious to a superficial observer of foreign manners but arises from the wish of all women to exalt the sentiment of the

passions—& to keep up the illusion which is their empire.—
Now D.J. strips off this illusion—& laughs at that & most
other things" (*BLJ* 8:148).

Thomas Moore, Byron's first official biographer, printed this
letter, and Guiccioli probably read it. Like his comic master-
piece, Byron's letters during his stay in Italy were filled with
laughter, facetiousness, and sexual bravado—all of which ap-
palled Guiccioli. This was the man she had to make a saint, a
man who jeered at sentiment,[30] and who was, in the words of
Paul West, "the raper of decorum."[31]

After Guiccioli cut loose the albatross of his irony and irrev-
erence, Byron rose like a resurrected man, canonized by her
love. Her editorial exclusions sanctified both herself and her
subject and created for her the delightful illusion of a poet who
said just what she wanted him to say. She did not mention in
her *Recollections* their sexual assignations, for those incidents
would have toppled the illusion of Platonic love she had so art-
fully erected. But when she interleaved her recollections with
the testimony of *his* poetry, his delight in ironic detachment,
bathos, and anti-romantic ribbing often undercut her. Her bio-
graphical rule of thumb seemed to be "delete or be deleted."
the more she amplified Byron's perfections, the more she her-
self emerged as the subject of the biography.

In grooming Byron and herself for posterity, Guiccioli did
not stop at trimming his literary corpus; she had ingenious de-
signs for thinning out the man himself. The second half of her
chapter on Byron's antimaterialism and the quality of his soul
is taken up with a description of his diet. She tried to demon-
strate that just as Byron could not bear to see women eating or
drinking, he had very little appetite himself, and her habit of
deleting damning evidence produced some glowing reports of
his abstemiousness.

If Lord Byron's anti-sensuality were not sufficiently proved by his
actions, words, writings, and by the undeniable testimony of those who
knew him, it might still be abundantly proved by his habits of life, and
all his tastes; to begin with his sobriety, which really was wonderful. So

much so, that if the proverb, Tell what you eat, and I will tell you what you are, be true, and founded on psychological observation, one must admit that Lord Byron was almost an immaterial being.[32]

Guiccioli then cited examples from previous biographies to corroborate her view: how often Byron went to bed without supper, turned down a drink, or watered down his wine. From these testimonials she distilled his "rule of life": "the desire and resolution of making matter subservient to the spirit."[33] That this was the rule animating her own life and her recollections of Byron has been amply suggested already. But her efforts in the remainder of this chapter made explicit what had been only implicit in the way she gelded passages from *Don Juan* to fit her fantasies and moral agenda. Here, Guiccioli erased Byron's body. As a Christian she was well equipped to sacrifice the letter in order to vitalize the spirit; as a devout Catholic she accepted the doctrine of transubstantiation; and as a woman she could, according to Byron, "transfigure brighter than a Raphael." But perhaps in her representation of Byron's ascetic habits she invented a kind of lay analysis.

Guiccioli quoted from Moore's *Letters and Journals of Lord Byron with Notices of His Life* (1830) to prove that Byron practiced strict vegetarianism and believed that one behaves like the brutes one has eaten. Byron did in fact practice a kind of irregular vegetarianism, and particularly in his youth he seemed as preoccupied with his weight as any fledging cult figure.[34] Guiccioli took her evidence for his asceticism from material published in Moore's biography, and again she cited selectively to make a case for her man-saint. Here is Guiccioli citing Moore citing a Byron memorandum dated April 1814.

I have been fencing with Jackson an hour a day by way of exercise, *so as to get matter under, and give sway to the ethereal part of my nature* [Guiccioli's emphasis]. The more I fatigue myself, the better my mind is for the rest of the day; and then my evenings acquire that calm, that prostration and languor, that are such a happiness to me. Today I fenced for an hour, wrote an ode to Napoleon Bonaparte, copied it out, ate six biscuits, drank four bottles of soda-water, read the rest of the time.[35]

A prisoner in Guiccioli's text, Byron is on a strict diet of bread and water. She italicized his ethereal nature, overlooking contrary evidence in order "to get matter under." She did not mention, for example, a letter Byron wrote the next day to Moore.

I am but just returned to town, from which you may infer that I have been out of it; and I have been boxing, for exercise, with Jackson for this last month daily. I have also been drinking,—and, on one occasion, with three other friends at the Cocoa Tree, from six till four, yea, unto five in the matin. We clareted and champagned till two—then supped, and finished with a kind of regency punch composed of madeira, brandy, and green tea, no real water being admitted therein. [*BLJ* 4:91]

Nor could Guiccioli possibly stomach the animality and pointed irreverence of another passage from the same letter.

The other day I nearly killed myself with a collar of brawn, which I swallowed for supper, and indigested for I don't know how long;—but that is by the by. All this gourmandize was in honor of Lent; for I am forbidden meat all the rest of the year—but it is strictly enjoined me during your solemn fast. [*BLJ* 4:92]

What actually appealed to Byron about Catholicism, ironically enough, was precisely its palpability, a point he made in his letter to Moore dated March 8, 1822.

It is by far the most elegant worship, hardly excepting the Greek mythology. What with incense, pictures, statues, altars, shrines, relics, and the real presence, confession, absolution,—there is something sensible to grasp at. Besides, it leaves no possibility of doubt; for those who swallow their Deity, really and truly, in transubstantiation, can hardly find any thing else otherwise than easy of digestion. [*BLJ* 9:123]

Byron found the Catholic faith—so replete with the icons and rituals he seemed to enjoy in any form—aesthetically compelling. Catholicism alone made him swallow his deity. Guiccioli obviously found this material attraction and its flippant expression equally objectionable.

Guiccioli continued her digest of Byron's spiritual qualities and antimaterialism by discussing his appreciations of female beauty. She claimed that "Lord Byron could only admire for a moment material beauty without expression in women; it might give rise to sensation, but could never inspire him with the slightest sentiment."[36] She then connected the subjects of diet and female beauty, and delivered the opinion quoted in this chapter's epigraph. In her opinion, Byron's antipathy toward seeing a woman eat was the reflection of an ascetic virtue that *he* practiced and, moreover, a sign of his preference for women beyond "corporeal necessities." Guiccioli therefore justified Byron's treatment of women by attributing this singular preference to his own spiritual nature and to his love of others so formed, or rather unformed. One can think of her biographical technique in citing only the most ethereal moments from the Juan and Haidee episode as her attempt to put the poem on a diet in order to "get the [subject] matter under" control. An ascetic writer, she had the misfortune to be dealing with a poet who loved to "gourmandize" in honor of Lent.

Guiccioli went to great lengths to note Byron's annoyance "at having to descend from the sublime and tender heights to which his soul had risen, to the vulgar and prosaic details of material existence."[37] Byronic bathos, however, gambols gleefully in just this direction, a fact about Byron and his mock epic which she refused to see. The Byron myth she created resembles the legend that would grow up around the irretrievably skylarklike Percy Shelley.[38] But Guiccioli was not merely projecting pleasing illusions for her own edification. She was also trying to make Byron into a legend, and legends, presumably, must be as immaterial as she believed Byron liked his women to be. But at the end of her life Guiccioli conjured up the spirit of Byron and got a chance to do to him what he repeatedly did to women in his poetry, and sometimes in his life.

In her brief remarks on Byron's dramas *Sardanapalus* (1821) and *Heaven and Earth* (1821), Guiccioli confessed that one could not possibly do justice to these plays merely by quoting passages from them: "No quotation could convey an idea of the noble energetic feeling animating these two dramas, for adequate language is wanting; impervious to words, the sentiment they contain is like a spirit pervading, or a ray of light warming and illuminating them."[39] In the summer of 1866—forty-two years after Byron's death—she tried to establish a direct link with this spirit and thus transcend the problem of finding "adequate language." It was about this time that Daniel Dunglas Home, a native Scot who had become an American illusionist and medium, was putting on shows and holding séances in France and Italy and apparently introduced Guiccioli to the basics of communication with the dead. Her activities were part of a vogue of late nineteenth-century spiritualism, which, Alex Owen argues, "validated the female authoritative voice and permitted women an active professional and spiritual role largely denied them elsewhere." When Owen claims that "female mediumship was predicated in part on a nineteenth-century view of women as morally and spiritually refined creatures who were particularly suited to the negation of self which mediumship demanded," one thinks of Guiccioli's giving herself over to the spirit of Byron.[40] But certainly these sessions also formed an important part of Guiccioli's later fantasy life, a way of recalling the famous poet from the dead and making him say just the right things. It was Byron who suffered an odd kind of negation, a spiritual editing.

During her séances Byron's spirit would take control of Guiccioli's hand, a hand that no longer needed to expurgate the outpourings of the poet's soul, which had been, at long last, converted. As her second husband, the Marquis de Boissy, observed to her during a séance: "How gratifying for you that he is a Catholic at last." The marquis himself sometimes submitted a question to Byron through her and thereby garnered stock market tips. After the Marquis de Boissy died in 1866, Guiccioli apparently set up a correspondence with him as well and claimed that her late husband and Byron were the best of friends. In producing these volumes of automatic writing, she imbued herself with the very spirit of Byron. This form of communication with Byron's spirit also allowed her to transcend the problem of adequate language, for she had become the medium she sought.

Guiccioli's rapid transcribing of Byron's communiqués from the spirit world brings to mind an observation she made about the furious pace at which he composed *Don Juan*. According to Guiccioli, Byron admitted that while writing he was inhabited by "un mauvais lutin," and in a note on this remark, Erwin Stürzl cites a famous passage in a letter from Byron to Thomas Moore concerning their "art" of writing: "It comes over me in [a] kind of rage every now and then, like * * * *, and then, if I don't write to empty my mind, I go mad" (*BLJ* 8:55).[41] A writing/copulating machine, Byron composed himself, therapeutically, to stay sane. Guiccioli also practiced a kind of writing therapy, and she copulated, platonically speaking, with the very spirit of Byron—a spirit that now spoke French (the language of angels, said Guiccioli), despite the fact that Byron rarely spoke French while on earth. Her book of automatic writing both completed the transubstantiation initiated in her biography of Byron and commingled her own textual rages with those of her fantasy man.

Apparently, Guiccioli transcribed several volumes of spiritual communication with various departed friends. These books of automatic writing may have disappeared.[42] We do have secondhand evidence of her séances with Byron, however, in Mary R. Darby-Smith's "My Reminiscences of Madame la Marquise de Boissy." Darby-Smith was an American who made Guiccioli's acquaintance when the latter was communicating with her dead friends and lovers. The editor of the *Victoria Magazine* (published in London 1863–80) tells its readers in a note on the first page of the article: "We gladly afford an American lady an opportunity to relate her personal experience of one who has already been prejudicially brought before the public. We admire the fidelity and loyalty which urges the courageous vindication of a friend."[43] We must remember that eight years before the publication of this article Harriet Beecher Stowe's *Lady Byron Vindicated* had flayed Byron, and that Guiccioli's friend Lamartine had more recently produced a not completely flattering portrait of the poet. Just as Guiccioli's biography of Byron was meant to clear him of all the charges made in these earlier

works, so Darby-Smith's article heaped one encomium after an-
other on both of them. We learn from this piece that "Madame
De Boissy [Guiccioli] was a spiritist" and that she told Darby-
Smith she had "prayed so much for Lord Byron that he had
become elevated to an exalted state in heaven."[44]

Here is Darby-Smith's account of one session devoted to
"the accomplishment of my visit, to obtain a communication
from Lord Byron." (I have translated the French portions; see
Appendix A for a transcription of them.)

I shall never forget the scene that followed. She took down one of the
large square pamphlet-shaped books with a crimson cover. She opened
it, bent her fine classic head over her clasped hands, and was in prayer.
Then she sat silent for a moment and looking up, said, "He will speak
with us." She then made the sign of the cross on the paper at the head
of the dialogue that was to ensue. She asked him relative to me, and
his answer came, and then I ventured to ask some questions through
her mediumship. She was called a writing medium. The answers came
like magic, and were written down with utmost rapidity and facility.
They were so interesting to me, I remarked at the conclusion, I should
like to have them. With her accumstomed kindness, she at once said,
"I will copy them for you," which she did in French; and here they are
precisely at she wrote them for me, at least as much of them as I think
proper to extract from a little book which I have, and which I shall
ever value as a souvenir of her good nature, and of that pleasant and
remarkable evening.

The following answer came to a question put by her to Lord Byron.

Response: Yes, I see you with a very delightful lady, who under-
stands me better than my countrymen ever did. Tell her that I admire
her and that I am happy to see her with you, my dear Teresa.

This series of questions and answers contain much that I prefer not
repeating; but what I do give is the exact copy of her words.

Answers to Questions

Q: Will I see you?

A: Yes, you will be, one day, in heaven. . . .

Q: In heaven will I find him whom I will be able to love?

A: But that I am not allowed to say. These are mysteries whose
secret of God has not been revealed to us. However, I believe that,
having as great a heart as you do, you will find peace in heaven which

you lack on earth, because you have not been able to find a heart worthy of understanding you.

Q: She wants to leave for America. What advice do you have for her?

A: Yes, I advise her to put it off for a little while, so that she may write with greater certainty about her affairs. Then she will herself be able to without consulting me, to leave without fear of making a mistake.

Q: Have you nothing else to say to her?

A: Yes, I can tell her that everything that she shall do will always be worthy of a virtuous and generous heart. Nevertheless, she must walk on the path of justice and of religion, because only in this way can one find tranquillity on the earth, and happiness in eternity.

Q: Do you have anything else to tell her?

A: Why, no, except that I will always pray to the good Lord for her, that he grant her tranquillity on earth, and happiness in eternity.

Questions after the departure of M.R.D.S.

Q: Do you want to tell me all your thoughts about her?

A: Yes, she is goodness itself, but too enthusiastic about everything. This means that she spoiled her life, and that she was unable to get married, because she was unable to understand others, or to be understood.

* * * *

Now you are her idol. Her enthusiasm for me has redoubled since she became aware of you. She has a keen intelligence, but she suffocates it out of religious prejudices.

* * * *

Her conscience is one of the most pure on earth. She shall be one of the angels of our heaven when she dies, and she shall have very little to expiate. She passed over the earth without sullying herself.[45]

After presenting her abridged transcript of Guiccioli's automatic writings, Darby-Smith titillated her readers by alluding again to what she had not included: "This (by her accredited) conversation with Lord Byron I have written verbatim, omitting only what appeared to me obligatory on my part."[46] The author here echoed her earlier admission that the questions and answers "contain much that I prefer not relating." What she left out (and why) we shall probably never know, but presumably it was material that had no direct bearing on her own presence. As for what she did report, one can only say that the spirit of Lord Byron clearly must have found the straight and narrow path that had so eluded his corporeal being on earth. Indeed, his uxorious and pious demeanor would have pleased both Annabella Milbanke and Harriet Beecher Stowe.

In discussing Guiccioli's séances and the apparitions she claimed to see, Darby-Smith made an interesting reference to Walter Scott's *Letters on Demonology and Witchcraft* (1830), a work in which the author had, according to Darby-Smith, "related peculiar incidents, and given marvellous reports of supernatural visitations and unearthly sights and sounds, which no logic can reasonably explain."[47] This is the very work in which Scott refers to "the glamour, or *deceptio visus* . . . a special attribute of the race of Gypsies."[48]

It is a wonderful coincidence that Home, a Scot, first gave Guiccioli lessons in the occult. Her ability to conjure up Byron's spirit has suggestive affinities with "coisting the glamorye," but in her case the *deceptio visus* seems to be both a spell she put herself under, a self-seduction, and a performance that she put on for Darby-Smith's benefit. For Guiccioli clearly cast a spell over Darby-Smith just as Byron had cast a spell over her. One may go even further and suggest that Darby-Smith, our only source for this spiritual communication, may have been something of a conjurer herself. Like Guiccioli, she left out anything not completely flattering to all parties concerned. In doing so she could both enchant her readers and show off her connections to famous people, living and dead. She thus blended the occult and modern senses of glamour, a blend that Byron's own life had first shown to be possible.

Communicating with the spirit of Byron completed the dream vision occasioned by Guiccioli's first sight of him in 1819, when she claimed he appeared to her as a celestial apparition.[49] Guiccioli struggled to preserve this beautiful illusion in the face of Byron's devilishly material objections, and her biography of the poet represented a final triumph of spirit over matter, an escape from infernal allusions into paradisaical illusions. The Byron of Guiccioli's biography and her séances was a magnificently ethereal reproduction of the "original." Byron's forcing women to live in an "illusive environment" thus summoned a belated reprisal in Guiccioli's spiritualizing of *him*, for in séances they could converse without being "subject to vulgar corporeal necessities." Guiccioli thus achieved mastery over her subject and her subject matter. She found the notes toward this supreme fiction in her mental edition of, one might say, "The Recollected Works of Lord Byron," an edition that completely digested its material. To this volume of memory and desire she contributed her book of automatic writing. The Byron she conjured up—now a Catholic, a sentimentalist, and a speaker of French—became a most unlikely angel in the house.

Lawrence's portrait of Lady Blessington, reproduced by permission of the Trustees of the Wallace Collection.

5

The Art of Conversation: Lady Marguerite Blessington

Now, my *beau idéal* would be a woman with talent enough to be able to understand and value mine, but not sufficient to be able to shine herself.

—Byron to Lady Blessington

An author should be judged of by his works, rather than by his conversation; for the latter takes its colour from those with whom he converses; whereas his writings, being the fruit of solitude, bear the tint only of his own mind.

—Lady Blessington

If women were writers, Byron was usually ill-disposed toward them. If they were great talkers, so much the worse.[1] Though he could admire the writings of Madame de Staël ("her works are delightful"), he could not endure her forcing others "to listen & look at her with her pen behind her ear and her mouth full of *ink*" (*BLJ* 4:19). There is plainly a connection between his revulsion for women eating in front of him (both Annabella Milbanke and Madame de Staël were great gourmandes) and for women speaking voluminously. Women have traditionally been placed either above or below culture, deemed spiritual or animal but not rational. Byron inherited this brand of misogyny, yet he often seemed disturbed when women were either too spiritual or too animal: hence his aversion to Milbanke's piety and her appetite.

In Italy in 1823, Byron met a beautiful, superb conversationalist, one who could not only "shine herself" but, left to her own devices, outshine him. Marguerite, the Countess of

Blessington—one of England's most fashionable, self-made ladies— traveled with her husband and the redoubtable dandy Count D'Orsay to France in the summer of 1822. By the spring of 1823 the Blessington entourage had moved to Genoa, Blessington admitting in her diary that the greatest attraction was not the city.

> Desirous as I am to see Genoa the Superb, I confess that its being the residence of Lord Byron gives it a still greater attraction for me. His works have excited such a lively interest in my mind and the stories related of him have so much increased it, that I look forward to making his acquaintance with impatience. . . . I long to compare him with the *beau ideal* I have formed in my mind's eye and to judge how far the descriptions given of him are correct.[2]

As so often in the life of Byron, his reputation and literary images had preceded him, and the countess was clearly ready to record her disappointment in the man.

Blessington wasted little time arranging an introduction to Byron, and they soon afterward shared a number of horseback rides around Genoa and the countryside.[3] During these rides they had several long conversations which Lady Blessington noted in her diary. Four separate texts eventually emerged from their interviews: (1) notes and transcripts of conversations, March 1 to May 1 1823; (2) *Conversations*, serialized in the *New Monthly Magazine,* July 1832 to December 1833; (3) *Conversations* published in book form as *Journal of the Conversations of Lord Byron,* 1834; (4) *The Idler In Italy,* 1839. In a fifth text, *Desultory Thoughts and Reflections* (1839), the countess published a number of Byronic "reflections"—in both senses.[4]

Two gaps entered into these iterations: the first between the actual event of the conversations and Lady Blessington's notes on them (we do not know when she made these notes), the second between the time of the conversations and their first publication nine years later in the *New Monthly Magazine.* One would ordinarily not wish to make much of the first gap, but the sheer length (in final print) of the orations Blessington "remembered" suggests either that she had a bardic memory or that even in making notes in her diary she amplified many of Byron's remarks. It seems likely that in 1823 she made cursory notes shortly after conversing with Byron, and then embellished them dramatically in 1832 when she was called upon to publish these notes as full-blown conversations.

In 1839 Blessington attempted to recapture a sense of veracity in her earlier notes on Byron and their meetings by publishing the "MS. book"—her diary of her life and times in Italy—as *The Idler in Italy*.[5] In this work she deleted or abbreviated certain passages in order to make the record of her contact with Byron appear matter-of-fact and unadorned. Even Teresa Guiccioli, who attacked the serialized *Conversations* for their inaccuracies, indiscretions, and pure inventions, would admit that *The Idler in Italy* "est un livre charmant—et lorsqu'elle parle de Ld Byron on y retrouve le coeur et la vérité."[6]

Each version of the notes introduced greater instability into the textual situation and allowed greater latitude for Blessington's private interests and the tints of her own mind. Even though *The Idler in Italy* seemed to restore stability and veracity by paring away all but the "facts," one naturally wonders whether Lady Blessington, reacting to uneven reviews of the *Conversations* and Guiccioli's public hostility, did not partly fictionalize these presumably original diary entries. Such editorial retrenchments, however, concern me less than her first set of amplifications, those acts of conjuring that resulted in the serialized *Conversations* (1832–33) which were consolidated in the *Journal* (1834). For if Blessington was a charming confidante and hostess who was expert at making conversation with Byron, she was also an aspiring author, quite adept at *Conversation*-making. Despite what she said about an author's being "judged of by his works, rather than by his conversation,"[7] Blessington did, in fact, judge Byron in her modes of representing him in the *Conversations*, which was of course *her* work and the one by which, indeed, she has been judged, with varying degrees of sympathy.

Both contemporary and modern reviewers of the *Conversations* have allowed that Lady Blessington made shrewd observations on Byron's character, but most readers also noted how her personality and opinions colored those of her subject. R.R. Madden, Blessington's friend and biographer, tactfully faulted her on this score and identified a motive for her creativity.

With the strongest regard for Lady Blessington it cannot be denied that, whether discoursing in her salons, or talking with pen in hand on paper in her journals, she occasionally aimed at something like stage effects . . . or passed off appearances as realities. This was done with a view to acquiring esteem, strengthening her position in the opinion of persons of exalted intellect or station, and directing attention to the side of it that was brilliant and apparently enviable.[8]

Commenting on the *Conversations*, Doris Langley Moore justly observes:

Discourses running into pages on end are often so far out of [Byron's] character in opinions and expression that they cannot be supposed even accurately reconstructed, far less accurately remembered. They are interlarded everywhere with genteelisms, French words, and clumsy pedantries typical of Lady Blessington's style and highly untypical of Byron's.[9]

The mixture of praise and blame that characterized the reviews of her book has been summed up in Leslie Marchand's bibliographical synopsis: "A shrewd contemporary interpretation somewhat colored by the writer's personality."[10] Blessington would seem to have answered these criticisms in telling Dr. Madden that "she could have made them [the conversations] better, but they would no longer have been what they now are, genuine."[11]

Like Annabella Milbanke, Marguerite Blessington tried to mark her distance from Byron's beguiling self-representations and the heady appeal of his reputation. To underscore her detachment from the man and the legend, she strategically placed disclaimers for her apparent relish in recording the poet's unpoetic nature. "It is only Byron's preeminence as a poet that can give interest to such details as the writer has entered into: if they are written without partiality, they are also given in no unfriendly spirit; but his defects are noted with the same feeling with which an astronomer would remark the specks that are visible even in the brightest stars."[12]

Blessington both reverenced Byron from afar and inspected his grainy defects, giving many notices of his "star quality" even as she adjusted her lens and zoomed in for some unflattering close-ups. Her own fortune, fame, and power rely on her "spotting" (detecting and diminishing) the phenomenon "Byron." In her *Desultory Thoughts and Reflections*, she associated poetry with astronomy: "Poets make a book of nature, wherein they read lessons unknown to other minds, even as astronomers make a book of the heavens, and read therein the movements of the planets."[13] As an aspiring writer, Blessington read Byron like a book, but this book was the one she was writing. As an astronomer, she charted the movements of the planet that had moved into her ken, but it is not clear that she saw the forces magnetically attracting her or recognized that she was being, strictly speaking, influenced. Like Annabella Milbanke, she was partly under a spell she did not see. But unlike Milbanke, she partly put Byron under a spell he could not see, not by making conversation with him but by making his conversation. She wrote in her book of reflections that "conversation is the legs on which thought walks; and writing, the wings by which it flies."[14] As a result of her winged account of her interviews with Byron, a complex set of representations underpin the *Conversations*, an alternately glossy and grainy portrait of both the interviewer and the interviewed, a play of reflections and refractions that makes it difficult to tell who was the subject of whom.

Blessington conjured up lasting impressions of her "original" impressions. The initial event referred to in the serialized *Conversations* thus became preempted by the secret, transforming initiatives of the very person who constituted its first explicit audience. That Byron, at the time the conversations took place, was aware of her role is suggested by a remark he made in a letter about his connection to "this new Goddess of Discord": he referred to his commerce with Lady Blessington as being "literally literary" (*BLJ* 10:174). She was a goddess of discord

largely because of the tensions her presence occasioned in
Byron's relations with his Italian lover, who wasted no time in
despising the English lady. When Blessington's interviews were
first published, Teresa Guiccioli referred to them as "Imaginary
Conversations"—a particularly ironic indictment, considering
the kind of conversations she herself would have with Byron
forty years after his death.[15] For both Blessington and Guiccioli
the act of recollection was a connossieurship of englamored
moments. Unlike Guiccioli's conversations with an angelic
Byron, however, Blessington's took place on earth in physical
proximity to her subject, a subject who was quite willing to
play the devil for her.[16]

Both Byron and Blessington were aware that their interviews
had literary potential. Blessington claimed that Byron "affects
a sort of Johnsonian tone, likes very much to be listened to, and
seems to observe the effect he produces on his hearer."[17] Such
a pose called for a Boswell or a Piozzi to hear his eloquence, and
Lady Blessington made certain she was in the right place at the
right time. Her opening observations in the *Conversations*
cited two precedents for the project she had undertaken, antic-
ipating that she would later in her work highlight Byron's
Johnsonian posing.

The deep and general interest with which every detail connected with
Lord Byron has been received by the public, induced the writer to pub-
lish her Conversations with him. She was for a long time undecided as
to adopting this measure, fearful that, by the invidious, it might be
considered as a breach of confidence; but as Boswell's and Mrs. Piozzi's
disclosures, relative to Dr. Johnson, were never viewed in this light,
and as Lord Byron never gave, or implied, the slightest injunction to
secrecy, she hopes that she may equally escape such an imputation.[18]

Mrs. Piozzi (née Hester Lynch Salusbury) however, did fall prey
to a number of unflattering imputations. Readers of the Febru-
ary 1, 1786, edition of the *London Morning Herald*, for example,
could find the following announcement of Piozzi's long-awaited
anecdotes on the late Samuel Johnson: "Report frequently whis-
pered that a connubial knot would be tied between Mrs. Thrale

and Dr. Johnson;—that event never took place, and yet Mrs. Piozzi and the Doctor, it seems, are shortly to be *pressed* in the same *sheets*."[19]

This squib contains a number of literal—and literary—truths. After the death of Mrs. Piozzi's first husband, Henry Thrale, Johnson had had some hopes that he might successfully solicit the affections, and perhaps even the hand, of Thrale's widow. Although she spurned Johnson's connubial interest and married her Italian music teacher, Mrs. Piozzi understandably wished to share in the posthumous fame of England's most formidable man of letters. She wanted to be bound to Johnson textually: pressed in the same sheets as her subject. The journalist's remark suggestively combined sex and texts and metaphorically tied the knot that never got tied. Thus did Mrs. Piozzi's biographical ambitions become wedded to sexual feelings she never actually had for Dr. Johnson; indeed, she found him physically repulsive. One must remember that English high society treated her marriage to Gabriel Piozzi with scorn and derision and looked upon her retreat to Bath and then to Italy as an abandonment of Johnson during his last days. In fact, the general opinion of her published anecdotes was that they discredited their subject, and many detractors were quick to claim that Mrs. Piozzi presented uncomplimentary anecdotes about Johnson in order to rationalize her uncharitable behavior toward him. Just as Johnson sought (though perhaps less wittingly) to excuse his commerce with the dissolute Richard Savage by partly excusing his shortcomings, so Mrs. Piozzi sought to explain her own neglect of Johnson by not excusing his shortcomings.

Another major criticism of her work resulted from the public perception that she was merely exploiting her earlier relations with Johnson to achieve her own fame. In this sense, "to be pressed in the same sheets" meant being closely associated with his literary reputation, if only incidentally as an ear for his verbal flourishes and bon mots. That she rushed to publish these tidbits caused Boswell, the self-designated official biographer of Johnson, to complain endlessly of her presumption, inaccuracies, and malice in producing her anecdotes.

Boswell had long since considered himself "in bed" with his subject and made no attempt to disguise his literary ambitions. Their rivalry intensified when it became apparent that they were quite literally working along similar lines: that is, both relied chiefly on anecdotes in presenting some of Johnson's not-so-lovable eccentricities, and both had the audacity to comment on his physical peculiarities.

Boswell's *Journal of a Tour to the Hebrides with Samuel Johnson, L.L.D.* (1785) occasioned a furor because of its candid disclosures of Johnson's behavior. Horace Walpole called it a "most absurd enormous book. . . . It is the story of a mountebank and his zany."[20] In his biography of Mrs. Piozzi, James Clifford explains the hostile reaction to Boswell's journal: "The general public expected a biographical portrait to be formalized, and to be either panegyrical or openly antagonistic. This very human combination of merit and eccentricity was new and not wholly to their liking."[21] Like all biographers, Boswell and Piozzi were therefore rivals in how they chose to present their common subject. Both wanted to embalm Johnson for futurity and become famous in the process. Mrs. Piozzi must have been pleased that the same newspaper that had ridiculed her forthcoming work printed six numbers in a series of excerpts called, "Leaves collected from the Piozzian Wreath, lately woven to adorn the Shrine of the departed Dr. Johnson."[22] Her own laurels were woven into this wreath, thus fulfilling her dream of self-adornment. Lady Blessington likewise entwined herself around Byron's life for two months in 1823 and then wove a wreath of memories to adorn both his shrine and the shrine she was building for herself.

Referring to cult figures and idols during this period, Leo Braudy observes that "once the message of fame was sent out by their very visible careers, it could return in an incredibly expanded form."[23] In her conversations with Byron, Blessington participated in Byron's greatness and returned it in the expanded, embellished form of her *Conversations*. The countess may also be seen as carrying on an eighteenth-century desire to make, as Braudy says, "the fame of voices spoken into ears, the fame of *talk*, so long considered impermanent—into something permanent and even artistic."[24]

If Byron exploited the vogue of orientalism during his years of fame, Blessington exploited the commercial possibilities of a Byron legend that grew out of that fame. As Ernest J. Lovell flatly states, "The *Conversations of Lord Byron* was written because she needed money."[25] The pageant of memoirs, recollections, and biographies preceding it suggested that the time was ripe for Blessington to tap an emerging Byron legend and serialize her *Conversations*. Between Byron's death in 1824 and the publication of Blessington's *Conversations* in 1832, London booksellers had published at least eleven works.[26] Those most closely associated with Blessington's project include James Kennedy's *Conversations on Religion, with Lord Byron and Others, Held in Cephalonia* (1830), Thomas Moore's *Letters and Journals of Lord Byron, with Notices of His Life* (1830), and especially Thomas Medwin's *Conversations with Lord Byron: Noted during a Residence with His Lordship at Pisa, in the Years 1821 and 1822* (1824). Closest in spirit to Blessington's work, Medwin's *Conversations* presented a Byron whose speech resembled the letters he wrote from Italy during the period. That voice was already a recorded and remembered voice, of course, and Medwin came in for much abuse from critics and friends who pilloried him for his inaccuracies. As Hobhouse said to Mary Shelley, "I know more than half the conversations to be downright forgeries."[27]

Thomas Moore's biography, authorized by John Murray (rather than by Byron's family or executors), approached Byron through contemporary anecdotes and published the first large sample of letters and journals, parts of which he suppressed, silencing the voice that often delighted in indiscretions. Blessington invited Byron's indiscretions, but her stake in her subject altered what Ernest Lovell (quoting the *Iliad*) called "his very self and voice" by adding her own voice to his.[28] It is worth noting that in January 1846 the editors of the newly established (London) *Daily News* solicited Blessington's confidential services for "any sort of intelligence she might like to communicate, of the sayings, doings, memoirs, or movements in the fashionable world."[29] Madden states that these contributions "consist of what is called 'Exclusive Intelligence.'"[30] Her intelligence was "exclusive" in two senses. Blessington's conversations with Byron gave notice of Byron's character even as *her* intelligence partly excluded her putative subject. Like the biographical writings of Piozzi and Boswell, her work mixed panegyric and antagonism, merit and opprobrium. Like her two predecessors, she often seemed to be a mountebank, Byron her zany.

Blessington's initial view of Byron, recorded in diary form in the 1832–33 *Conversations* ("Genoa, April 1st, 1823"), set the tone for her debunking of the legend that bore his name.

Saw Byron for the first time. The impression of the first few minutes disappointed me, as I had, both from the portraits and descriptions given, conceived a different idea of him. I had fancied him taller, with a more dignified and commanding air; and I looked in vain for the hero-looking sort of person with whom I had so long identified him in imagination.[31]

Of this first meeting, Blessington later wrote in her diary: "Well, never will I allow myself to form an ideal of any person I desire to see; for disappointment never fails to ensue."[32] Once disappointed, Blessington idealized no more; on the contrary, she often imagined the worst of her subject after he had squashed her high expectations. Her reflection in her diary showed that she had lost her desire to form a *beau idéal*, a desire she presumably sacrificed in 1823 when she first encountered the "reality" of the man who had become the source of so many fantasies. Indeed, having met Byron, she could say of him what he had said at the beginning of his masterwork: "I want a hero."

By inspecting Byron's worst personal traits, Blessington repeated the program of systematic disenchantment Byron himself offered in *Don Juan*. That is, she became expert at turning "what was once romantic to burlesque" and in doing so, ensured that the Byron legend would no longer easily seduce those who saw it only from a distance. She characteristically put words in Byron's mouth.

As it is said that no man is a hero to his valet-de-chambre, it may be concluded that few men can retain their position on the pedestal of genius *vis-à-vis* to [sic] one who has been behind the curtain, unless that one is unskilled in the art of judging, and consequently admires the more because she does not understand. Genius, like greatness, should be seen at a distance, for neither will bear a too close inspection.[33]

One of Blessington's "desultory thoughts" confirmed this view: "Mountains appear more lofty, the nearer they are approached; but great men, to retain their altitude, must be viewed only from a distance."[34]

Vis à vis Lady Blessington, who would seem highly skilled in the art of judging, even Byron's remarks on the problem of over-exposure suffered overexposure. Like Boswell and Piozzi before her, Blessington ceremoniously violated the privacy of her subject. Writing on Boswell's depiction of Johnson, Patricia Spacks observes: "As a private man, the hero resembles other men. Intimate specificity modifies the myth of heroism. Gossip emphasizes what people hold in common, dwells on frailties, seeks the hidden rather than the manifest; heroism thrives on specialness and on public manifestation."[35] These remarks hold true also for Blessington's treatment of Byron, although she would claim that *he* dwelt on his frailties more than anybody and that she was merely making public his private views. She thus forestalled criticism of her own disclosures by showing Byron's insistence on fully exposing himself. But two entries in her "Night Thoughts Book" (1834) show her self-consciousness about this kind of criticism: "Those who cannot exalt themselves, are prone to pull down others, hence the world will always be filled with Levellers"; and "We never more fully display our own characters than when we assail those of others."[36] The countess summarized these thoughts in the epigram "Calumny is the offspring of Envy."[37] She thus anticipated the deglamorizing of famous people best represented in our day by Kenneth Anger's *Hollywood Babylon* (1975),[38] which sensationalizes the defects of our favorite movie stars, and Paul Johnson's *Intellectuals* (1988), a book exposing the moral hypocrisy and scandalous personal lives of such favorite authors as Rousseau, Shelley, Marx, Tolstoy, and Sartre.

One of Blessington's most deflating reports of Byron's person appears early in the *Conversations* when she is describing his clothing and horsemanship: "His appearance on horseback was not advantageous, and he seemed aware of it, for he made many excuses for his dress and equestrian appointments. . . . He did not ride well, which surprised us, as, from the frequent allusions of horsemanship in his work, we expected to find him almost a Nimrod."[39] Here Blessington lashed the heroes of the oriental tales with the whip of *Don Juan*. But she regularly projected onto Byron precisely the defects and affectations to which she herself was most prone. When she wrote, for example, "I never met with anyone with so decided a taste for aristocracy as Lord Byron, and this is shown in a thousand ways," she displayed one of her own most striking characteristics. As Doris Langley Moore affirms "By an all but unconscious irony, there is scarcely a failing of which Lady Blessington accused Byron which was not contemned in herself—triviality, self-love, vanity of rank, sententiousness, insincerity, affectation, coarseness, talking too much—and making an excessive use of coronets!"[40]

Like Blessington, Byron had an uneasy relation to aristocratic privilege, and as a result both developed a taste for ostentation that betrayed their nervousness about rank and status. Like Byron, Blessington knew how to puncture romantic fantasy images. In this role as a comic iconoclast, she resembled the narrator of *Don Juan* and thus subjected Byron to the kind of abuse his mock epic so memorably presents. The passage on Byron's unheroic horsemanship was, ironically enough, followed by a discussion of how best to guarantee that one's reputation will not suffer at the hands of one's "friends." Again we find ourselves in a conversational conundrum, for it is difficult to tell whether Blessington faithfully recorded Byron's words or partly invented his spirited diatribe in order to cast aspersions on the biographical maltreatment in which she had just indulged.

I should have positively destroyed myself, but I guessed that —— or —— would write my life, and with this fear before my eyes, I have lived on. I know so well the sort of things they would write of me—the excuses, lame as myself, that they would offer for my delinquencies, while they were unnecessarily exposing them, and all this done with the avowed intention of justifying, what, God help me! cannot be justified, my *unpoetical* reputation, with which the world can have nothing to do! One of my friends would dip his pen in clarified honey, and the other in vinegar, to describe my manifold transgressions, and as I do not wish my poor fame to be either *preserved* or *pickled*, I have lived on and written my Memoirs, where the facts will speak for themselves.[41]

Unfortunately, some of his friends, afraid that Byron's memoirs would present just this "unpoetical reputation," would burn those texts and thus create a vacuum that Blessington's *Conversations* hoped partially to fill. "I have written my Memoirs," Blessington recounted Byron's saying, "to save the necessity of their being written by a friend or friends, and have only to hope they will not add notes."[42] Those who were disappointed that Byron's memoirs went up in smoke thus found in Blessington's journal of conversations a substitute for the inside stories they never got to see in print, stories she generously interleaved with notes of her own. Like the early biographers (particularly Thomas Medwin), Lady Blessington was too shrewd not to see the opportunity that the burning of the memoirs afforded her, and so she dipped her pen by turns in honey and vinegar in describing her subject.[43] The long-running illusion she presented was that her *Conversations* was a document of her candor, equivalent in spirit and letter to the seemingly unedited outpourings of Byron's masterpiece and his most private journal.

Pretending to be offended by Byron's unmannerly and even reckless confessions, Blessington nevertheless had no compunction about publishing them and then morally editorializing upon the poet's squibs, particularly those designed to wound his friends and acquaintances.[44] Blessington wrote: "Talking of this gift [the Memoirs] to Moore, he asked me if it had made a great sensation in London, and whether people were not greatly alarmed at the thoughts of being shown up in it? He seemed much pleased in anticipating the panic it would occasion, naming all the persons who would be most alarmed."[45] Affecting to be the champion of the maligned, Lady Blessington offered a delightfully underhanded response to Byron's gleeful slander that shows *him* up.

> I told him that he had rendered the most essential service to the cause of morality by his confessions, as a dread of similar disclosures would operate [more] in putting people on their guard in reposing dangerous confidences in men, than all the homilies that ever were written; and that people in the future [would] be warned by the phrase of "beware of being *Byroned*," instead of the old cautions used in past times. "This (continued I) is a sad antithesis to your motto of *Crede Byron.*" He appeared vexed at my observations, and it struck me that he seemed uneasy and out of humour for the next half-hour of our ride.[46]

This is one of Lady Blessington's most elaborately constructed depictions of Byron's character. Her presumably lighthearted quip about "being *Byroned*" could not have been better designed to vex him, for having read Thomas Moore's biography of him, she knew how seriously he took the family motto. Indeed, Moore cited an incident from his childhood in which, fittingly enough, the young Byron made good on a promise to throttle a schoolmate who had earlier insulted him. "On his return home, breathless, the servant inquired what he had been about, and was answered by him, with a mixture of rage and humour, that he had been paying a debt, by beating a boy according to promise; for that he was a Byron, and would never belie his motto, 'Trust Byron.'"[47]

One could always trust Byron to get his revenge, either by slugging or by slander. Since Blessington thought that Byron was not telling "*the whole truth,*" but rather lied about his friends, she saw his disclosures as representing only "a sad antithesis" to his alleged trustworthiness. To her mind, then, "beware of being *Byroned*" meant "beware of confiding in Byron, for he will betray your trust in him."[48]

Blessington's decision to report nearly all of Byron's disclosures and her avidity in "getting the dirt" on her buttonholed celebrity suggest that, for his part, Byron should have been wary of being *Blessingtoned*. In having Byron act mortified by her seemingly casual remark, she put him into a funk and then graciously released him from it.

I told him that his gift [of confession] to Moore suggested to me the following lines:—

> The ancients were famed for their friendship we're told,
>   Witness Damon and Pythias, and others of old;
> But, Byron 'twas thine friendship's power to extend,
>   Who, surrender'd thy Life for the sake of a friend.

He laughed heartily at the lines, and, in laughing at them, recovered his good-humour.[49]

After letting Byron stew for a good half-hour, Blessington had simply changed the subject, the talent he celebrated as Lady Adeline's miraculous sense of tact.[50] Blessington's turn of mind effortlessly refigured the significance of Byron's gift of his "Life" (his memoirs) and found in it the material for some good-natured lines about the poet's generosity—lines he greatly admired.

These lines, however, allegedly spoken on the eve of his departure, also commemorate Byron's Greek campaign and his heroic death.[51] This generous prolepsis shows Lady Blessington's fabricating hand in the text and suggests that she gladly compromised verisimilitude in order to offer her genuine praise for a man to whom a nation entrusted its revolutionary interests (such as they were). In making up these lines, as if on the spot, Blessington also improvised even as she demonstrated that, for her, Byron did live up to his family motto after all. The entire scene thus elaborately concocted the conditions for Blessington's display of humanitarianism, tact, and poetic ability. But the exchange also celebrated the poet by magnifying the life he was shortly to lay down for his comrades in Greece.

That both Byron and Blessington were conscious of this mutual desire for self-glorification is suggested by a remark of his that she recorded.

Byron does not like contradiction: he waxed wroth today, because I defended a friend of mine whom he attacked, but ended by taking my hand, and saying he honoured me for the warmth with which I defended an absent friend, adding with irony, "Moreover, when he is not a poet, or even a prose writer, by whom you can hope to be repaid by being handed down to posterity as his defender."[52]

This wry observation doubles over with irony. As authors, Byron and Blessington were each in a position to hand the other down to posterity, and also in a position either to defend or defame the other's character. In reproducing this remark for her readers, Blessington promoted herself as a disinterested, noble soul who stood up for her friends. She called attention to this benevolence by having Byron commend her for it. But such passages—and there are many in the *Conversations*—also show off her talent for calling attention to the double acts of celebration and criticism in which she was engaged. She appears no less conscious than Byron of the power, in this case the commemorative power, of writing. Indeed, she seems to be calling attention to this aspect of her dealings with Byron precisely in order to forestall the criticism that she was turning his gossip into her glamour. This particular remark involves her in a complex game of mirroring, a game to which she added her later reflections and self-imaging ambitions when her notes became the *Conversations*. We will see just how complicated this mirroring can be in her mode of representing her verbal interplay with Byron.

Blessington often mirrored her subject in a way that was nothing short of poetic, as Byron observed:

Poets (and I may, I suppose, count myself among that favored race, as it has pleased the Fates to make me one), have no friends. On the old principle that "union gives force," we sometimes agree to have a violent friendship for each other. We dedicate, we bepraise, we write pretty letters, but we do not deceive *each other*. In short, we resemble you fair ladies, when some half dozen of the fairest of you profess to love each other mightily, correspond so sweetly, call each other by such pretty epithets, and laugh in your hearts at those who are taken in by such appearances.[53]

Byron's confession invited Blessington to acknowledge that, like poets, women gaily deceive others but never one of their own kind. She politely demurred, but she may very well have been rescripting her reaction to Byron's self-debunking in the shadow of her own cynical views on human nature. Whose attack on female deviousness was this? Blessington would have all her readers taken in by Byron's "compliment," but as with so many of the opinions she "reported," this one has the ring of truth—or perhaps the pleasing chime of two half-truths. Byron's notorious left-handedness had no idea what Blessington's right hand was up to. She thus practiced an art that Byron celebrated in *Don Juan*:

> Now what I love in women is, they won't
> Or can't do otherwise than lie, but do it
> So well, the very truth seems falsehood to it. [*CPW* 5:476]

The narrator of *Don Juan* asserts that a lie is nothing but "the truth in masquerade," and that one cannot state a fact "without some leaven of a lie." Blessington presented the truth about Byron and herself in the masquerade of her persuasive falsehoods, and in this sense she unconsciously mirrored his playful subversion of the opposition of truth and lies.

It is often difficult to determine where Lady Blessington's character and views leave off and where Lord Byron's begin. Fluid speakers, they flow together. It is interesting that Blessington referred to Byron's lack of self-command and indiscretion as "a natural incontinence of speech"—precisely the charge he typically made against women who, like Madame de Staël, spoke voluminously. But in having Byron hold forth in presumably uncharacteristic ways (if his other biographers are to be at all trusted), Blessington partly scripted his logorrhea and, in doing so, gave herself a pretext for commenting on the very habit she helped to fabricate.

According to Teresa Guiccioli, Byron stooped to converse with the countess only in order to study her for Lady Adeline's shifty character in the English cantos of *Don Juan*.[54] But Blessington also appeared to be making a case study of Byron's *mobilité*.

He has a habit of mystifying, that might impose upon many; but that can be detected by examining his physiognomy; for a sort of mock gravity, now and then broken by a malicious smile, betrays when he is speaking for effect, and not giving utterance to his real sentiments. If he sees that he is detected, he appears angry for a moment, and then laughingly admits that it amuses him to *hoax* people, as he calls it, and that when each person, at some future day, will give their different statements of him, they will be so contradictory, that *all* will be doubted—an idea that gratifies him exceedingly! The mobility of his nature is extraordinary, and makes him inconsistent in his actions as well as in his conversation.[55]

And later she wrote:

Byron is a perfect chameleon, possessing the fabulous qualities attributed to that animal, of taking the color of whatever touches him. He is conscious of this, and says it is owing to the extreme *mobilité* of his nature, which yields to present impressions.[56]

If Guiccioli was right, and if Lady Blessington's observations about Byron's character were accurate, then the *Conversations* presents the spectacle of dueling, conversing chameleons—a contest of verbal showiness and shiftiness that make a hoax of the very possibility of candor, stable meanings, and sincerity as traditionally conceived.

Mobilité reworks sincerity as susceptibility to immediate impressions, a spontaneous overflow disclosed in the excitement of the moment. In a note to *Don Juan*, Byron glosses the term.

In French, "mobilité." I am not sure that mobility is English, but it is expressive of a quality which rather belongs to other climates [Irish?], though it is sometimes seen to a great extent in our own. It may be defined as an excessive susceptibility of immediate impressions—at the same time without *losing* the past; and is, though sometimes apparently useful to the possessor, a most painful and unhappy attribute.[57]

We should recall that the narrator of *Don Juan* refers to mobility as that "vivacious versatility / Which many people take for want of heart" (*CPW* 5:649). Such versatility makes Byron, Michael Cooke argues, the "consummate chameleon poet, changing themes and schemes quicker than the mind, let alone the eye, can follow."[58]

When Blessington and Byron are at one point trading favorite epigrams, it comes as no surprise that both delight in her version of an epigram by Samuel Rogers: "[Ward] has no heart they say, but I deny it: / He has a heart—he gets his speeches by it." The ever versatile Blessington amends this to suit an acquaintance of hers: "The charming Mary has no mind they say; / I prove she has—it changes every day."[59] Of Lady Adeline, the narrator of *Don Juan* says:

> She also had a twilight tinge of "Blue,"
> Could write rhymes, and compose more than she wrote;
> Made epigrams occasionally too
> Upon her friends, as every body ought. [*CPW* 5:634]

But Lady Blessington's "impromptu" verse would seem to echo Juan's complaint about the caprice of

> all women of whate'er condition,
> Especially Sultanas and their ways;
> Their obstinancy, pride, and indecision,
> Their never knowing their own minds two days.
> [*CPW* 5:334]

This talent for mind- and verse-changing and the ability to play "all and every part" (*CPW* 5:649) both enchant and unhinge Juan.

> Juan, when he cast a glance
> On Adeline while playing her grand role,
> Which she went through as though it were a dance,
> (Betraying only now and then her soul
> By a look scarce perceptible askance
> Of weariness or scorn) began to feel
> Some doubt how much of Adeline was *real*.
> [*CPW* 5:648; original emphasis]

The dance of social appearances that Adeline performs for a mostly unsuspecting public resembles Byron's own self-conscious, sometimes scornful choreographing of his poetic and personal images. Although Lady Blessington was a kindred spirit, or specter, in this pursuit, she affected a scorn of social thespianism. In her "Night Thoughts Book" she wrote: "The great majority of men are actors, who prefer an assumed part to that which nature had assigned them. They seek to be something, or to appear something which they are not, and even stoop to the affectation of defects, rather than display real estimable qualities which belong to them."[60] She also wrote: "The noblest characters only shew themselves in their real light; all others act comedy with their fellow men, even unto the grave."[61]

Again, Blessington's remark seems transparently self-reflexive. Madden observes that "she lived, in fact, for distinction on the stage of literary society before the footlights, and always *en scene.*"[62] Like Adeline, Blessington knew how to dispense "her airs and graces," but unlike Adeline, she was not "too well bred to quiz men to their faces" (*CPW* 5:650). In the *Conversations*, as we have seen, she often displayed her ability to nettle Byron into silence: she knew how *not* to make conversation when she wished to demonstrate the profound effect her wit and candor sometimes had. Blessington's later reflection on "politeness" bears mentioning: "A substitute for goodness of heart."[63] Adeline, on the other hand, agrees to "wear the newest mantle of hypocrisy" that lets her "restore [Juan] to his self-propriety" (*CPW* 5:635). The importance of *mobilité*, improvisation, and role-playing energizes both *Don Juan* and the *Conversations* and suggests the seam separating hypocrisy and sincerity in them.

For Byron, hypocrisy that set others at ease was not only benign; it was benevolent. Enlightened hypocrites, that is, know how to change the subject for the sake of comforting others; they also know how to change themselves *as* a subject in order to be, as the narrator says of Don Juan, "insinuating without insinuation" (*CPW* 5:593). Such hypocrisy, however, must be supremely self-conscious of its artifice, or it quickly degenerates into the fatuousness Byron called cant. Juan, we should remember, is also expert at playing *his* grand role both as a Russian ambassador and as a preternaturally modest figure who "had, like Alcibiades, / The art of living in all climes with ease" and who "neither brook'd nor claim'd superiority" (*CPW* 5:592, 593). For Blessington, on the other hand, Byron's *mobilité* revealed him as a shifty character always on the verge of some hypocrisy.

Like Guiccioli and Milbanke before her, Blessington read Byron's "mock gravity" as a sign of his annoying tendency to *mis*represent himself. After claiming that he "is vexed when he discovers that any of his little *ruses* have not succeeded," Lady Blessington amplified her opinion of his guile.

The love of mystification is so strong in Byron, that he is continually letting drop hints of events in his past life: as if to excite curiosity, he assumes, on those occasions, a look and air suited to the insinuation conveyed: if it has excited the curiosity of his hearers, he is satisfied, looks still more mysterious, and changes the subject; but if it fails to rouse curiosity, he becomes evidently discomposed and sulky, stealing sly glances at the person he has been endeavoring to mystify, to observe the effect he has produced. On such occasions I have looked at him a little maliciously, and laughed, without asking a single question; and I have often succeeded in making him laugh too at those mystifications, *manquée* as I called them.[64]

Blessington, however, often identified with these conversational obliquities and subterfuges, the art of being "insinuating without insinuation," a fact Guiccioli was quick to seize upon when she read the *Conversations*.[65] We should recall that Annabella Milbanke thought *Manfred* was designed "to perplex the reader, exciting without answering curiosity."[66] The same might be said of Blessington's expanded diary, although she intended it precisely to answer those curiosities about Byron's character which his own works had so mischievously excited. None of these three women wished to believe that Byron's chameleonism and contradictory nature represented his own brand of honesty, what one might call "the new sincerity," even if—as in Blessington's case—they subconsciously found this versatility enticing. Byron's new sincerity was distinguished from the old sincerity in having a deliberately, or perhaps reflexively, bad memory and an agile sense of humor. What others saw as moral slipperiness, Byron championed as a fidelity to the immediate.[67] The new sincerity surpassed the old sincerity in its commitment to change shape in accordance with the demands of immediate impressions.

Improvisation—the art of saying, with the narrator of *Don Juan*, "what's uppermost, without delay"—is closely related to this form of sincerity. Such freedom shows off "a conversational facility, / Which may round off an hour upon a time" (*CPW* 5:594). Indeed, when the narrator of *Don Juan* says in Canto 15, "I rattle on exactly as I'd talk / With any body in a ride or walk" (*CPW* 5:594), we may well remember that Byron's rides with Blessington took place during this same period. The narrator's admission seems to be an allusion to Byron's own capacity for rattling, a capacity to which Blessington's highly discursive *Conversations* also bears testimony. By underscoring his improvisational shiftiness, her *Conversations* therefore echo the way Byron wrote *Don Juan*. Blessington herself broached the issues of textual mimicry when she reported Byron's comments on his own face and his personal deformities, for his responses led her to speculate about the liberality and ease with which he transformed the work of other authors into his own.[68] In commenting on Byron's profound lack of anxiety about influences, Lady Blessington subconsciously called attention to her own textual transformations, mirrorings, and plagiarisms.

Byron, according to the countess, had his own views of his face. In one of the most telling bits of candor recorded (or created) in the *Conversations*, Blessington showed Byron playing his own physiognomist.

I have read, that where personal deformity exists, it may be traced in the face, however handsome the face may be. I am sure that what is meant by this is, that the consciousness of it gives to the countenance an habitual expression of discontent, which I believe is the case; yet it is too bad (added Byron with bitterness) that, because one had a defective foot, one cannot have a perfect face.[69]

Blessington ratified this observation: "He indulges a morbid feeling on this subject that is extraordinary, and leads me to think it has had a powerful effect in forming his character."[70] She reported Byron's claim that *The Deformed Transformed* resulted from his discontent with his own body, but Blessington reminded him that "in the advertisement to that drama, he had stated it to have been founded on the novel of 'The Three Brothers.'"[71] According to Blessington's text, Byron apparently ignored this reminder and immediately changed the subject, an evasion that led her to speculate on the nature of his lack of anxiety about literary influences: "It is possible that he is unconscious of the plagiary of ideas he had committed; for his reading is so desultory, that he seizes thoughts which passing through the glowing alembic of his mind, become so embellished as to lose all identity with the original crude embryos he had adopted."[72] Byron, that is, automatically transformed whatever he read and made it his own.

Like Byron, Blessington may have been unconscious of the "plagiary of ideas" she had committed in her *Conversations*, filtering the poet's thoughts through the alembic of her mind. After claiming that Byron's "is a fine nature, spite of all the weeds that may have sprung up in it," for example, she went on to offer rhapsodic observations on her subject's impressive defects.

Had his errors met with more mercy, he might have been a less grand poet, but he would have been a more estimable man; the good that is now dormant in his nature would have been called forth, and the evil would not have been excited. The blast that withers the rose destroys not the thorns, which often reeain, the sole remembrancer of the flower they grow near; and so it is with some of our finest qualities,— blighted by unkindness, we can only trace the faults their destruction has made visible.[73]

Like Milbanke before her, Blessington showed her fondness for Byron's imagery in *The Corsair* ("There grew one flower beneath its rugged brow").[74] Unlike Annabella, the countess did not acknowledge her borrowings, perhaps because, like Byron, she could not keep track of all the material she had adopted.

When Blessington wrote of Byron's character, "I am convinced that it is the excellence of the poet, or rather let me say, the effect of that excellence, that has produced the defects of the man," we must recall—as she doubtless did—the second stanza from Canto 16 of *Don Juan*.

> The cause of this effect, or this defect,—
>   "For this effect defective comes by cause,"—
> Is what I have not leisure to inspect;
>   But this I must say in my own applause,
> Of all the Muses that I recollect,
>   Whate'er may be her follies or her flaws
> In some things, mine's beyond all contradiction
> The most sincere that ever dealt in fiction. [*CPW* 5:619]

Byron was clearly alluding to Polonius, as was Blessington through (as it were) the alembic of the narrator's mind. One can think of her as tapping Byron's muse, who "treats all things, and ne'er retreats / From any thing" in order to produce her own "wilderness of the most rare conceits" (*CPW* 5:619). Chief among them was the conceit that while Byron was a shameless plagiarist, she was a faithful recorder of his conversations, rather than a quite brilliant, self-enchanting muse unto herself, one who also had the leisure to inspect the cause and number of Byron's defects.

Just as he deformed previous works, then, so she transformed his "original crude embryo" for her own purposes. Once again, Blessington's *Desultory Thoughts and Reflections* contains a telling analogue in a section headed "Effects Of Contact with Genius":

It is doubtful whether we derive much advantage from a constant intercourse with superior minds. If our own be of equal caliber, the contact is likely to excite the mind into action, and original thoughts are often struck out; but if any inferiority exists, the inferior mind is quelled by the superior, or loses whatever originality it might have possessed, by unconsciously adopting the opinions and thoughts of the superior intelligence.[75]

This thought too may very well have been gleaned from Byron, but it is possible that it belonged to Blessington, who possessed a superior mind of her own—a mind not easily quelled by Byron's, as she often showed in the *Conversations*. The question of who was plagiarizing whom again raises its hydra head. Blessington seems to have had the kind of consciousness that she denied to the inferior party, but in this case both minds of "equal caliber" seem only vaguely conscious of their powers of influence.

Blessington's caliber of mind matched her interlocutor's, and thus she could not resist the temptation to "shine herself." Autobiography ineluctably spilled over into her portrait of Byron, suggesting that the *Conversations* offers the fictional voice-from-beyond-the-grave associated by Paul de Man with the trope "prosopoeia." De Man argues that prosopoeia "is the trope of autobiography, by which one's name . . . is made as intelligible and memorable as a face."[76] Like Wordsworth's *Essays upon Epitaphs*, Blessington's ostensible tribute to Byron runs into autobiography, and the figural conundrums that result from this confluence bear on the phenomenon of mirroring and deformation which I have been examining. De Man's remark that "the autobiographical moment happens as an alignment between the two subjects involved in the process of reading in which they determine each other by mutual reflexive substitution"[77] applies to the way Blessington "reads" Byron's conversation and to her unconscious and self-formative alignments with her subject, whom she reads like a book (the book she is writing).

Sometimes their mutual substitutions appear lucidly self-reflexive. Blessington reported Byron's observation that "we are least disposed to overlook the defects we are most prone to," and to his question: "Do you think as I do on this point?"[78] she replied: "As a clear and spotless mirror reflects the brightest images, so is goodness ever most prone to see good in others; and as a sullied mirror shows its own defects in all that it reflects, so does an impure mind tinge all that passes through it."[79] To this shrewd comment, "Byron laughingly said, 'That thought of yours is pretty, and just, which all pretty thoughts are not, and I shall pop it into my next poem.'"[80] In fact, he did, and perhaps even in direct reference to Lady Blessington: "Sweet Adeline, amidst the gay world's hum, / Was Queen-bee, the glass of all that's fair" (*CPW* 5:528). Yet it is impossible here to determine who is deforming whom, for perhaps Blessington read Byron's depiction of Lady Adeline, saw her own image reflected in it, and popped *his* thought into her *Conversations*. Was Blessington Byron's "clear and spotless mirror," prone to see his good qualities, or was she a "sullied mirror," staining and deforming "all that passes through it"? In this nexus of speculation and citation the future of an allusion is undecidable and variously authored, a Foucaultian dream of "subject-functions" jockeying for position in a discourse that has no origin and no end.

Plagiarism, biography, autobiography, defacement, and mirroring crystallize in Byron's praise of John Curran and in the exchanges that ensued. Byron, according to Blessington, recalled

[Curran's] once repeating some stanzas to me, four lines of which struck me so much, that I made him repeat them twice, and I wrote them down before I went to bed:

> While Memory with more than Egypt's art
> Embalming all the sorrows of the heart
> Sits at the altar which she raised to woe,
> And feeds the source whence tears eternal flow!

I have caught myself repeating these lines fifty times; and, strange to say, they suggested an image of memory to me, with which they have no sort of resemblance in any way, and yet the idea came while repeating them; so unaccountable and incomprehensible is the power of association. My thought was—Memory, the mirror which affliction dashes to the earth, and, looking down upon the fragments, only beholds the image multiplied.[81]

This thought may have been conjured up from Blessington's unfragmented memory of Canto 3 of *Childe Harold*.

> Even as a broken mirror, which the glass
> In every fragment multiplies; and makes
> A thousand images of one that was,
> The same, and still the more, the more it breaks
> And thus the heart will do which not forsakes,
> Living in shattered guise, and still, and cold,
> And bloodless, with its sleepless sorrow aches,
> Yet withers on till all without is old,
> Shewing no visible sign, for such things are untold.
>
> [*CPW* 2:88]

Indeed, Blessington's *Conversations* was a series of fragments multiplying Byron's image (his reputation) and mirroring his poetic images. As such, it also set up a glass in which Lady Blessington would see herself and—through her many (written) reflections—we her.

Blessington expertly avoided witting duplicity by humbling herself before Byron, but even this maneuver called attention to herself. After offering an encomium on his thoughts about memory and fragments, she demonstrated her own powers of association.

I told him that his thoughts, in comparison with those of others, were eagles brought into competition with sparrows. As an example, I gave him my definition of memory, which, I said, resembled a telescope bringing distant objects near to us. He said the simile was good; but I added it was mechanical, instead of poetical, which constituted the difference between excellence and mediocrity, as between the eagle and the sparrow. This amused him, though his politeness refused to admit the verity of the comparison.[82]

Like a mechanical simile, Blessington's definition no sooner courted comparison with Byron's than she automatically passed an unfavorable judgment on it; she brought Byron close to her only to observe her relative mediocrity. Like Byron, however, her memory was governed by the incomprehensible "power of association." Indeed, Blessington's memory was a telescope bringing Byron closer to her readers, her work a series of fragments multiplying not merely her memories of their conversations but also her opportunities for soaring on the wings of her writing.

Sixteen years after her conversations with Byron and seven years after producing the *Conversations*, Blessington reached a sad conclusion about a certain kind of female fantasizing.

Women, with their bright imaginations, tender hearts, and unsullied minds, make unto themselves idols, on which they lavish their worship, making their hearts temples, in which the false God is adored. But, alas! the Idol is proved to be of base clay, instead of pure gold, and though pity would conceal its defects, and cherish it even with them, Virtue, reason, and justice destroy the false Idol, but in doing so, injure forever the temple where it was enshrined.[83]

Blessington learned how to enshrine her imagination and literary talents instead of flesh-and-blood idols. Even as she gazed into the night of her thoughts, her writings represented a source of new self-enchantment, a site on which her imagination secretly disported with itself, changing the subject—and Byron as her subject—at will. She imagined a "Byron" who, unlike Teresa Guiccioli's saint, seems more lame than the original, but she also gave notices of his life, work, and personality that show both his genius and hers—or rather, his genius through the glowing alembic of her mind. In making a production out of Byron, Blessington magically fused the gracious, mobile art of making conversation and the labored, artfully made *Conversations*.

She thus decreated and recreated the legend that had partly formed her. The *Conversations* sometimes seem a kind of literary revenge against the man whose *beau idéal*, he claimed, was a woman far less talented than the one to whom he expressed this very opinion. If Byron did not say this, then Lady Blessington cleverly invented the context in which to show off her talent. Against Byron's perfect woman, who would value him but be unable to "shine herself," Blessington offered the shimmering ingenuity of her *Conversations*. This work deglamorized Byron (in the modern sense) and yet also—oddly, in spite of itself—bore out Lady Blessington's definition of sympathy.

Each thought of mine an echo found in his:
Our minds were like two mirrors placed on walls
Fronting each other, and reflecting back
The self-same objects,—such is sympathy.[84]

This mirroring represents a benign version of what Milbanke saw as the malignancy of Byromania: the aping of Byron's seductive poses. Unlike Milbanke, Blessington wished less to reform than deform Byron. But her deeper attraction to Byron's thoughts and to many of the images in his poetry revealed an unconscious form of identification that suggestively belied her pointed criticisms of him. The hall of mirrors the *Conversations* presents often makes it impossible to see who was identified with or deforming whom. If Lamb could, as Byron admitted, imitate his hand to perfection and therefore produce forgeries, Blessington could forge the very heart of Byron.

It seems fitting to conclude with the closest thing Byron wrote as a tribute to women unimpressed by his fame. The narrator of *Don Juan* describes the imperiously cool Aurora Raby, a woman not easily seduced by the poem's hero, thus:

Juan was something she could not divine,
    Being no Sibyl in the new world's ways;
Yet she was nothing dazzled by the meteor,
    Because she did not pin her faith on feature.

His fame, too,—for he had that kind of fame
    Which sometimes plays the deuce with womankind,
A heterogeneous mass of glorious blame,
    Half virtues and whole vices being combined;
Faults which attract because they are not tame;
    Follies trick'd out so brightly that they blind:—
These seals upon her wax made no impression,
Such was her coldness or her self-possession. [*CPW* 5:605]

Byron also had that kind of fame. If he strongly disliked women such as Aurora Raby (whom some believe to be based on Milbanke), he nevertheless admired those who did not easily succumb to his meteoric reputation. He fed as much on the resistance of women as on their idol worship. Forging his hand and following his every move, as Lamb did, were acts of imitation Byron at first found intriguing, then boring, and finally contemptible. Milbanke piqued his interest that night in 1812 by not reacting—biologically or literarily—at all, by staying away from the shrine of Childe Harold and from the mesmerizing delusions of the imagination, and by pinning her faith on the features of a reformed husband. Byron's bright vices eventually enchanted her, and she warmed up to the idea that perhaps her shimmering virtues could do the same thing to him. But she could no more understand Byron than he could fathom a woman who would speak to him from beyond the grave in the voice of his dead Thyrza. Guiccioli fully divined him only as he spoke to her from heaven as a spirit wholly virtuous, his vices cannily edited, his spirit completely in her hands. Blessington handled Byron's image in such a way that he emerged from her *Conversations* as a grown-up version of the "fat, bashful boy" Elizabeth Pigot had long before described and rather liked. Yet his bright follies, endued with Blessington's memory and desire, no longer played the deuce with womankind—not, at least, with this kind of woman.

APPENDIX A

Transcription of French Portions from a Séance with Byron

Response.—Oui, je vous vois avec très-excellente femme, qui me comprend plus que mes compatriotes ne m'ont jamais compris. Dites-lui que je l'aime, et que je suis heureux de la voir auprès de toi ma bonne Thérèse. . . .

ponses aux Demandes.

Demande.—Vous verrai-je?

Response.—Oui, vous serez, un jour, dans le ciel.

Demande.—Trouverai-je dans le ciel celui que je puisse aimer?

Response.—Mais cela ne m'est pas donné de dire. Ce sont des mystères dont Dieu ne nous révèle pas le secret. Cependant, je crois qu'ayant un grand couer comme vous avez, vous trouverez le contentement dans le ciel ce qu'il ous manque sur la terre, car vous n'avez pu trouver un coeur digne de vous comprendre.

Demande.—Elle désire partir pour l'Amérique. Quels conseils lui donnez vous?

Response.—Oui, je lui donne le conseil de trainer encore un peu—afin que l'Amérique en lui écrive—des choses plus positives sur ces affaires. Alors elle pourra meme, sans me consulter, prendre son parti sans craindre de se tromper.

Demande.—N'avez vous rien d'autre à lui dire?

Response.—Oui, je puis le dire que tout ce qu'elle fera sera toujours digne d'un coeur honnê et généreux. Cependant, elle doit marcher dans le voie de la justice et de la religion, car c'est dans cette voie seulement que l'on peut trouver le repos sur la terre, et le bonheur dans l'éternité.

Demande.—Avez vous autre chose à lui dire?

Response.—Mais non, si ce n'est que je prierai toujours pour elle le bon Dieu afin que qu'il lui donne le répose sur la terre, et le bonheur dans l'éternité.

Paris, 27 Mars, dix heures du soir.

Questions apres le depart de M.R.D.S.

Demande.—Veux-tu me dire toute ta pensée sur elle?
Response.—Oui, elle est la bonté même, mais trop enthousiaste en toute chose. Ce qui fait qu'elle a gaté sa vie, et n'a jamais pu se marier, car jamais elle n'a pu [prendre] les autres, ni être comprise.

*   *   *   *

Maintenant tu-es son idole. Son euthousiasme pour moi est redoublé depuis qu'elle t'a connue. Elle a une belle intelligence, mais elle la suffoque sur les préjugés religieux.

*   *   *   *

Sa conscience est tout ce qu'il y a de plus pur sur la terre. Elle sera un des anges de notre ciel lorsqu'elle mourra, et elle aura bien peu à expier. Elle a passé sur la terre sans se salir.

APPENDIX B

The Byron Legend in an Age of Artificial Intelligence

Amanda Prantera's novelistic fantasy, *Conversations with Lord Byron on Perversion, 163 Years after His Lordship's Death* (1987), is the most recent contribution to the strain of Byromania I have been examining. Prantera's fictional conversations between a computer programmer (named Anna) and a program (named LB for Lord Byron) present the favorite images, illusions, idioms, symbols, mysteries, and rumors associated with this legend by feeding all of them into a computer capable of Artificial Intelligence (AI) or, more precisely, Cognitive Emulation. Such emulation is the technological equivalent of Byromania—the conspicuous aping of the Byronic routine of narcissism, seduction, and deception which Paul West has also recently captured, with a kind of horrific brio, in his novel *Lord Byron's Doctor* (1989).[1] In Prantera's fiction, a computer has been programmed to "emulate" Byron's intelligence by responding to the programmer's questions. The irony here rests with the fact that a woman, a Byron specialist, has programmed the computer and therefore made herself complicit in the responses she elicits: "It [the program] had what the female assistant called a 'richly structured semantics of the self,' the structure and the richness being of her own devising."[2] This reciprocal programming is one we have already seen in Byron's textual intercourse with women.

Prantera's computer expert exploits the possibilities of responding to the program she has created with a zeal and ingenuity that matches Teresa Guiccioli's or—and this is certainly Prantera's model—Marguerite Blessington's. Prantera cites the long tradition of Byromania of which her novel is a part by indicating where the professor in charge of this AI experiment got his funding: "Recently, though, having just received a large cheque from the honorary secretary of an organization called the ULBL—the Universal League of Byron Lovers (of which category, by the way, there seemed to be as many members, if not more, than there were when his Lordship was alive to reciprocate their affection)—funds had been less worry to him."[3]

Still at large 163 years after his death, Byron is wanted dead or alive, but clearly he is more valuable as an object of fantasy when he no longer exists to frustrate or parody those who seize on him. To put it another way, Thyrza is to Byron as Byron is to the women who fashion his legend: an occasion for emulation, narcissism, and fantasy, a locus of glamorous possibilities. We should recall that both Caroline Lamb and Annabella Milbanke made use of the Thyrza material in order to barter their way into Byron's sad heart. They were on the right course. In Thyrza, Byron saw the pleasing lineaments of his own desire, just as in Astarte, Manfred found an image of himself. These lineaments, the blood lines of the Byron legend, extend to our day in works such as Prantera's, where the issue of Byron's "perversion" becomes modified by the computer language it has been programmed to speak.

The question central to Prantera's book, therefore, the intrigue at the heart of the computer software, is the identity of Thyrza. The researchers in the story (not all of them either computer specialists or Byromaniacs) pitch the question at the most prurient level: "Was Britain's most renowned womanizer just another of our island's fairies?" (p. 13). Anna, the programmer, understands that the matter is "a bit more complex than that" (p. 13), and the greater part of the novel consists of her questions to "LB" and its enigmatic, often pettish rejoinders. After Anna asks a series of particularly leading questions, she switches the computer to "output only," a function that allows the program to "browse along of its own accord printing out reams of what looked to be a fairly good approximation to unspoken thoughts" (p. 24). In this mode, LB prints out its remembrances of things past and—at long last—reveals the story of Thyrza.

In telling this story, Prantera fabricates a richly whimsical account of Byron's erotic foreplay with Edleston and of his later confession to Percy Shelley about the affair. She supports her tale with all the apocryphal material about Byron's irregular life at Cambridge, but she also interpolates and exaggerates episodes in order to offer a truly mischievous solution to the mystery of Thyrza's identity. Prantera cleverly sets up her grand fiction about the true story of Byron and Edleston by allowing LB to complain about the sentimentality of biographical treatment. "Most of the biographers, he could see, didn't seem to have grasped this side of the question fully; they seemed to take it as a simple matter of fact that he'd been prone from the start to what they breezily dismissed as 'sentimental friendships' with young and pretty members of his own sex" (p. 98).

Prantera knows whereof she writes. Following Leslie Marchand's treatment of the subject in his three-volume biography of Byron, Jean Hagstrum has sentimentalized and spiritualized Byron's liaison with Edleston. He attaches great importance to the word "pure" in Byron's presumably definitive confession that his friendship with Edleston was "a violent, though *pure*, love and passion." Thus Hagstrum can conclude that Byron's feelings for Edleston "represented moral nobility and emotions as close as Byron ever came to religious exaltation."[4] Louis Crompton finds in the same material presumptive evidence for his claim that Byron was a practicing homosexual.[5] Prantera apparently can countenance neither the apotheosizing of Thyrza nor the homosexualizing of Byron. Her fiction heterosexualizes both parties by turning Thyrza into the girl everyone thought she was and then by inventing some sex scenes to impurify Byron's avowed passion. These scenes represent Prantera's fantasy of a Byron who was decidedly not one of her island's fairies.

Prantera's computerized Byron tells of a swimming episode in which he allegedly saved Edleston from drowning—and after which he discovered the truth about both Edleston and himself. The two were stretched out on the bank of a glade when the young lord discovered that the Cambridge choirboy had—*mirabile dictu*—breasts!

Not very full ones mind you, he decided on closer inspection; not much of a setting for the rubies; cups rather than cupolas; but very definitely breasts: two springy little hillocks—firm, fleshy, pretty as shells.

He held his breath and stretching out a fore-finger brushed it cautiously over the tip of the breast: it concentrated to a point, as if drawing itself to attention—a breast in full working order. Well flay me alive and sunburn me, he thought to himself in stupefaction! No wonder Edleston sang like a cherub, blushed like a peach and retained a marble-smooth jawline. No wonder he refused to swim in company and kept his shirt on when he did. Edleston was a hermaphrodite. [pp. 134–35]

Prantera cannot resist adding more voltage to this shocking recognition scene.

Wait a minute, though. Wait a *minute*: was he even that? And still more cautiously he drew the exploring hand downwards, piqued rather than otherwise by his discovery. . . . His hand

delved deeper into the secret recesses of Edleston's lower belly
and thighs. Yes, totally unnecessary. For as far as he could make
out through the layers of cloth that separated his index finger
from what lay underneath, Edleston was not a hermaphrodite,
nor even a eunuch: Edleston was a woman. [p. 135]

Byron's contemporaries believed Thyrza *was* a young woman, so in
one sense Prantera's fabulous fiction does no more than ratify this
belief by making Edleston/Thyrza female after all. Like truth itself,
Edleston is in masquerade, her sexual identity leavened with the lies
that come, Byron thought, so naturally to women.

This scene also seems to be partly cribbed from the end of Byron's
Lara (1814), in which the disguised Kaled's sexual identity is finally re-
vealed as "he" swoons over the dead body of Lara.

> He did not dash himself thereby, nor tear
> The glossy tendrils of his raven hair,
> But strove to stand and gaze, but reel'd and fell,
> Scarce breathing more than that he lov'd so well.
> Than that *he* lov'd! Oh! never yet beneath
> The breast of man such trusty love may breathe!
> That trying moment hath at once reveal'd
> The secret long and yet but half-conceal'd;
> In baring to revive that lifeless breast,
> Its grief seem'd ended, but the sex confest;
> And life return'd, and Kaled felt no shame—
> What now to her was Womanhood or Fame? [*CPW* 3:252–53]

When, late in the novel, Prantera's Byron tells Shelley the true
story of Edleston, the latter expresses understandable incredulity.

"Eureka!" said Shelley, his battle lost, dabbing helplessly at his
eyes. "Some discovery. I don't believe a word."
    "And why not, may I ask?"
    "Because it's too good to be true: a royal princess dressed as a
choirboy, beautiful as Antinous, wise as Athena, and with the
flair of a Newton in the bedchamber! You're making the whole
thing up." [p. 160]

Indeed, Prantera is, but her fiction interestingly falls into the line of
textual fantasies the Byron legend excites in those who purvey it. The
computer program's triumph of cognitive emulation takes its place in

the long series of Byronic forgeries and fantasies, many of them prefig-
ured by the poet's own images and self-images.

At the end of the novel, LB writes a love poem, a purportedly un-
programmed creation of its own.

> I have followed your shadow, o'erstepping your shade
> I have lived, I have loved, that our love would ne'er fade;
> And in places grown dark to me, calling your name,
> I have courted your likeness, or ghosts of the same.
>
> Your voice and your laugh and the curve of your breast
> (The one place on earth where my heart has found rest),
> I have sought them and found them and lost them apace;
> And I'd lie if I said I'd no joy in the chase.
>
> But believe me, if ever my words have been true,
> In the images, traces, and mirrors of you,
> In each heart I have plundered, each lip I have kissed,
> It was you I was seeking and you that I missed. [pp.173–74]

This poem is mysteriously addressed "To A——a," and we know that
Prantera's Byron enjoys calling Edleston "Alba" (a variant of "Albe,"
what Byron's Pisan friends nicknamed him). In Prantera's fiction, the
circuit of desire therefore includes the author, whose first name
(Amanda), happily enough, begins and ends in "a." Just as the Byron
expert programs LB, so the novelist programs her novel so that
through the agency of the programmer, Anna, she becomes one pos-
sible object of the poet/program's concluding love lyric.

Prantera ends the novel by having Anna try to puzzle out the pos-
sible addressees—a thoroughly Byronic game: "Augusta? Unlikely.
Annabella? Impossible. To who then? that was something she would
have to think about. To her, anyway, it didn't seem a bad poem at all.
On the contrary, she thought it was beautiful. Full of significance, if
only she could work it out, and very, very moving" (p. 174). The pro-
grammer blithely passes over the obvious choice—herself, Anna—
because this would be too good to be true. She might have recalled
that early in her probings the following exchange had taken place. LB
asked:

BY THE WAY DO YOU HAVE A NAME BESIDES A NUMBER?
ANNA.
AH, GOOD. It printed brightly: I LIKE NAMES THAT BEGIN AND END
WITH AN A. [p. 29]

If the slippery reference fits, wear it. Like Byron's verse, particularly his early love verse, Prantera's LB poem swivels around to face any one of a number of "A——a" names. The program itself tries to limit the number to two: "He could think of her [Anna] for a start. In fact he might even entitle the verses he was about to write 'To A——a,' and see if they wouldn't do double duty: put his mind to rest about Alba and get him off to a good start with this other young woman." (p. 171).

One recalls Byron's coy reply to Annabella when she queried him about the 1814 poem "Stanzas for Music" ("I speak not—I trace not— I breathe not thy name"): he said, "Perhaps I was thinking of you when I wrote that."[6] Indeed, LB's love poem seems to continue the mystery of referentiality surrounding "Stanzas for Music," a poem laced with hints of illicit love and traces of a guilty past. Byron—and Prantera has him pegged here—is a master tracer. His delight in tracing the contour of a promising female breast parallels but inverts his tendency *not* to trace, speak, or breathe the name of his beloved. Innuendo is the art of producing seductive traces. A trace is the place where fantasy rises to meet language, as flesh rises beneath a caress. "Thyrza" is such a trace, as is "Astarte." These proper names signify variously and draw readers into fantasies of self-attribution. "To A——a" offers a faint, therefore compelling, outline, and Prantera's novel ends with the programmer, like so many before her, mesmerized by the game of reference that Byron—and LB—so alluringly play. The stroke of the pen makes thousands, perhaps millions, fantasize.

In Prantera's work the grammar of Byronic glamour tricks itself out in the language of computers. Prantera seduces herself and her readers with the pleasing speculation that Thyrza was in fact a young woman, and her novel culminates with a poem that flirts with all women whose names begin and end in "a." Prantera's Byronic poem brings to fruition the penchant for fantasy and forgery. The whole of her in- vented "conversations" demonstrates that the appeal of cognitive emulation is particularly strong when the mind to be emulated is as giving of fantasies as Byron's. He intensifies self-enchantment by no longer existing to undermine its designs. Like most popular idols, Byron is more valued dead than alive.

Notes

INTRODUCTION

1. Sir Walter Scott, *The Complete Poetical Works* (Boston: Houghton Mifflin, 1900), p. 32.

2. Sir Walter Scott, *Letters on Demonology and Witchcraft*, 2d ed. (London: G. Routledge and sons, 1885), p. 87.

3. Cf. John Finlay, *Scottish Historical and Romantic Ballads* (Edinburgh: James Ballantyne, 1808), p. 39.

4. *The Compact Edition of the Oxford English Dictionary* (1971), s.v. "glamour."

5. The creators of *Glamour* magazine preserve the more "glamorous" (i.e., British) spelling, and (unconsciously) capitalize on a commercialized version of *deceptio visus* in the form of all those deceptively beautiful women they present, women whose images gypsy-photographers manufacture and then cast like spells over consumers hungry for airbrushed, poreless hallucinations. But the demystification of "glamour" is suggested by one of their own articles. The September 1989 issue advertises on its cover the article: "How To Make Good Skin Great Skin." Once a matter of supernatural bedazzlement cast from the outside, glamour then becomes a matter of *personal* aura radiating from the inside, and finally degenerates into our current practice of "reading" (about) the latest spells dreamed up by the cosmetics industry and then applying glamour, like rouge, to our faces. For a suggestive remythologizing of the "glamourpuss," see Roland Barthes "The Face of Garbo," in *Mythologies*, trans. Annette Levers (New York: Hill and Wang, 1972), pp. 56–57.

6. "Enid," ll. 740–43, in Alfred Tennyson, *The Complete Poetical Works*, 2 vols. (Cambridge: Cambridge Univ. Press, 1879), p. 221.

7. H. Rider Haggard, *Cleopatra* (London: Longmans, 1889), p. 110.

8. In *Heart of Darkness* (1899; Norton Critical Edition, ed. Robert Kimbrough [New York: Norton, 1988], p. 55) Joseph Conrad uses the word "glamour" four times, associating it with youth and exotic adventures. But the word is nuanced in each case to suggest a quest both gallant and futile. Referring to the Russian harlequin, Marlow says, "Glamour urged him on, glamour kept him unscathed."

9. *Webster's Third New International Dictionary of the English Language* (1976), s.v. "glamour."

10. Throughout this book I refer to these women by their last names. In doing this I deliberately breach the convention of referring to them only by their first names or titles, a convention that both trivializes and sentimentalizes their importance and writings.

11. Ralph Milbanke, Earl of Lovelace, *Astarte* (London: Christophers, 1905), p. 100.

12. Jean Baudrillard, *Seduction* (New York: St. Martin's Press, 1990), p. 69.

13. Ethel Colburn Mayne, *Enchanters of Men* (New York: Methuen, 1905), p. 215.

14. It is probably no accident that Byron's seductive glamour and Franz Anton Mesmer's theory of animal magnetism enjoyed a popular vogue contemporaneously. Byron's so-called "underlook" was his trance-producing version of what would become, largely as a result of Mesmer's research, the science of hypnotism.

15. Margot Strickland, *The Byron Women* (London: Peter Owen, 1974), p. 9.

16. See also Austen's cautionary "review" of Byron's *The Giaour* in *Persuasion*, ed. R.W. Chapman, 3d ed. (London: Oxford Univ. Press, 1933), pp. 100–101.

17. Edward John Trelawny was a bewildering blend of adventurer and raconteur who attached himself to Byron and his circle in Pisa, from 1821 to Byron's death in 1824 in Greece. In her journal, Mary Shelley called him "un giovane stravagante—partly natural and partly perhaps put on." Trelawny's autobiography, *Adventures of a Younger Son*, makes his life seem every bit as exotic and heroic as the *Corsair* of Byron.

18. Frederic Raphael, "The Byronic Myth," *Byron Journal* (London), no. 12 (1984): 78–79.

19. Ibid., p. 83.

20. Camille Paglia, *Sexual Personae: Art and Decadence From Nefertiti to Emily Dickinson* (New York: Vintage Press, 1991), p. 351.

21. Quoted from one of Caroline Lamb's letters (recipient unnamed) in *"To Lord Byron": Feminine Profiles Based upon Unpublished Letters, 1807–1924*, ed. George Paston and Peter Quennell (New York: Scribner's, 1939), p. 84.

22. I am thinking of Philip Martin's *Byron: A Poet before His Public* (Cambridge: Cambridge Univ. Press, 1982), a work whose promising title I would like to make good on by putting Byron and his poetry directly before some of his readers.

23. One need hardly point out that Harold Bloom's treatment of literary influence is restricted to men ("strong poets"). It is interesting that Bloom's revisionary ratios have nothing to say about Byron. A comprehensive theory of influence must take into account all the influences shaping an author's work, not merely the monumental, clubbable ones. Cf. Harold Bloom, *The Anxiety of Influence* (New York: Oxford Univ. Press, 1975).

24. Jerome Christensen, "Byron's Career: The Speculative Stage," *English Literary History* 52 (1985): 72; revised in Christensen, *Lord Byron's Strength* (Baltimore: Johns Hopkins Univ. Press, 1993), pp. 142–84. I am indebted to Christensen's shrewd insights about the production of "Byron" by his readers.

1. TRIAL FANTASIES

1. Although past sixty when Byron met her in 1812, Lady Melbourne enchanted him and became his confidante during his years of fame. She introduced him to Lady Caroline Lamb, wife of her son William, and acted as a go-between for their tumultuous affair. Lady Melbourne later passed along his proposal to her niece, Annabella Milbanke.

2. Quoted in Leslie Marchand, *Byron: A Biography* (New York: Alfred A. Knopf, 1957), 1:82.

3. *Letters of an Italian Nun and an English Gentleman* (Harrisburg, Pa.: John Wyeth, 1809). This edition is, E.H. Coleridge believes, probably a forgery (see his *Works of Lord Byron* [London: John Murray, 1898], vol. 1, p. 15). The thirty-one letters tell the story of Mr. Croli's (the English gentleman's) courtship of Isabella, the Italian nun. In an early letter he hopes to find "the avenues of [her] heart less impregnable than the walls of the convent," and she responds by admitting that she is "not formed for a monastic life. . . . My mind cannot confine itself within the walls that surround its mistress." Mr. Croli and Isabella go back and forth like this for roughly half the book, and both construct elaborate arguments, proposals, and counterproposals. Isabella is certain that Croli's interests are fleeting ("You will soon lose the temporary image of a beauty which never had much to boast"), and he counters with a vow of constancy ("My mind is so deeply impressed with your image, that it is not susceptible to any other"). The situation reaches a pathetic stalemate when the desparate Croli plants himself in a cottage next to the convent "to behold the temple which contains the idol of my heart, though I could not be admitted to it." He finally loses all hope of extracting Isabella from the nunnery, and suddenly finds himself at sea and—worse—kidnapped by pirates. His failure to answer Isabella's letters grieves her terribly and, upon his miraculous return, she agrees to join him in England, where she expects to be married. An elated Mr. Croli returns to England and charts his beloved's progress out of Italy and finally to London. There Isabella discovers, however, that Mr. Croli cannot obtain the blessing of his peers and so will retain her only as a mistress. She is mortified, and her worst suspicions about Croli's false promises are confirmed. She writes a letter to his mother disclosing these events, returns to Italy, and receives permission to enter a Neapolitan abbey, where she remains for the rest of her life. Croli writes a moving suicide note to his mother and then kills himself. Isabella never learns of his fate.

4. Quoted in Willis Pratt, *Byron at Southwell* (Austin: Univ. Of Texas Press, 1948), p. 14.

5. The end of "L'Amitie est l'amour sans ailes" also bears citing.

> Fictions and dreams inspire the bard
> Who rolls the epic song;
> Friendship and Truth be my reward—
> To me no bays belong;

> If laurell'd Fame but dwells with lies,
> Me the enchantress ever flies,
>   Whose heart and not whose fancy sings;
> Simple and young, I dare not feign;
> Mine be the rude yet heartfelt strain,
>   'Friendship is Love without his wings!' [*CPW* 1:25]

I don't think the enchantress ever flew far.

6. Jerome McGann, "'My Brain Is Feminine': Byron and the Poetry of Deception" *Byron: Augustan and Romantic*, ed. Andrew Rutherford (London: Macmillan, 1990), pp. 26–51.

7. Ibid., p. 14.

8. Pratt, *Byron at Southwell*, p. 15.

9. Ibid., p. 16. Interestingly enough, this nun is named "Isabella," which is Annabella Milbanke's middle name. The book also foreshadows Byron's liaison with Teresa Guiciolli, who was no nun, though she was educated in a convent.

10. Quoted in Pratt, *Byron at Southwell*, p. 16.

11. Rousseau, *Letters*, p. 16.

12. Megan Boyes, *Love without Wings: A Biography of Elizabeth Pigot* (Derby: J.M. Tatlen, 1988), p. 3.

13. See *BLJ* 7:117.

14. Quoted in Pratt, *Byron at Southwell*, p. 38.

15. The most thorough account of this event appears in Doris Langley Moore, *The Late Lord Byron* (New York: Harper & Row, 1977), chap. 1.

16. I discuss this Virgilian translation and the importance of these alterations later.

17. See George B. Walsh, *The Varieties of Enchantment: Early Greek Views of the Nature and Function of Poetry* (Chapel Hill: Univ. Of North Carolina Press, 1984), pp. 107–26, 160 n. 5.

18. If Teresa Guiccioli was Byron's "last attachment," then Mary Chaworth was his first and, some think, fatal attachment—the girl whose rejection of him discolored his later relations with women.

19. Paston and Quennell, *To Lord Byron*, p. 7. This book, like *The Gallery of Byron Beauties*, (London: Tilt and Bogue. 1836), contains a gallery of women, and the letters the editors select, though they are real, mostly idealize both the women and the romantic poet to whom they write. Thus, the women remain in profile, like Elizabeth's silhouette. Missing from this collection are the letters of Augusta Leigh, Lady Byron (Annabella Milbanke), and Lady Melbourne.

20. Elizabeth wrote: "There was a youth in the Choir, when Ld. Byron was at Cambridge, with whose voice he was much charmed, that he frequently had him at his rooms. and grew so fond of his society, from his amiable disposition and pleasing manners, that he provided for him by placing him in an advantageous Mercantile concern—he died of consumption at an early age, his name was Eddelston, and this poem was written upon his giving Ld. Byron a small Cornelian heart when he left Cambridge." See McGann's, note to poem no. 87, *CPW* 1:381.

21. In Paston and Quennell, *To Lord Byron*, p. 9.

22. See *BLJ* 1:124, 8:24; and Marchand, 1:107–8).

23. Ralph Milbanke, *Astarte*, p. 100: "Byron was curiously addicted to imitating anything that might impress him as a literary image of himself." I believe that this addiction was widespread, with Byron both its transmitter and reflector.

24. See *BLJ* 1:125 n. 2.

25. "Bulldog" was also a contemporary slang word for a college servant accompanying a proctor, "who is responsible for the behaviour of undergraduates, on his rounds" (William Freeman, *A Concise Dictionary of English Slang* [London: English Universities Press, 1955], p. 37). This meaning, however, seems to have no place in the context of Elizabeth's remarks.

26. See Byron's preface to *The Corsair* (*CPW* 3:148) for one of his most colorful protests against these predictable identifications.

27. Michel Foucault, *The History of Sexuality*, trans. Robert Hurley (New York: Vintage Books, 1988), 1:35.

2. BYRON'S MINIATURE WRIT LARGE

1. Quoted in Strickland, *The Byron Women*, p. 53.

2. This forgery appears in facsimile form in John Murray's two-volume edition of *Lord Byron's Correspondence* (London: John Murray, 1922), pp. 130–31. It has not, to my knowledge, been subsequently reprinted, or transcribed, in whole or in part.

3. I am indebted to Cecil Lang for deciphering the words underneath the scribbling; the last lines read: "My Dearest Friend take care of this if you can but believe me your devoted & most trusted servant. Yours most truly." That this was a conventional closing to letters of the period makes Caroline's scratching it out seem even more peculiar. But I would argue that she simply wrote in the standard closing and then purposely scribbled over it, in imitation of Byron's habit, to make the forgery appear more authentic.

4. Peter Manning, in *Byron and His Fictions* (Detroit, Mich.: Wayne State Univ. Press, 1978), writes of "the hysterical strain generally permeating her conduct (p. 85)." Byron's conduct during his affair with her seems no less "hysterical," if that dangerous word must be used.

5. Strickland, *The Byron Women*, p. 11.

6. Lady Oxford had married Edward Harley, fifth Earl of Oxford, in 1794 when she was twenty-two. A free spirit in politics and love, she had several affairs, including a brief one with Byron in 1812, as he grew weary of Lady Caroline's indiscretions. Lady Oxford went abroad in 1813 with her husband, but Byron did not follow her.

7. Caroline temporarily enjoys the position of Byron's "monstrous double," to use another Girardian term, but the traffic of letters, miniatures, and forgeries is so heavy in this affair that the "triangle of desire" must mutate in order to make sense of it all. Cf. René Girard, *Violence and the Sacred*, trans. Patrick Gregory (Baltimore: Johns Hopkins Univ. Press, 1977), chapter 6.

8. This comedy of eros and mimesis brings to mind another of Girard's observations on the form of desire he so intriguingly examines: "Man cannot respond to that universal injunction, 'Imitate me!' without almost immediately encountering an inexplicable counterorder: 'Don't imitate me!' (which means, 'Do not appropriate *my* object'). . . . Neither model nor disciple really understands why one constantly thwarts the other because neither perceives that his desire has become the reflection of the other's."

9. As a young woman Lady Melbourne had been sexually precocious but apparently less visibly so than Lamb. Byron's letters sometimes flatter her by suggesting that she would have made a fool of him had he known her in her hot youth. I have not included Lady Melbourne as a "handler of Byron's image" in this book, but she clearly played an important role in the social construction and advertising of Byron's reputation, aura, and notoriety. She was a willing partner in his fame and a silent one in his infamy.

10. A point of information: Byron has spared me the task of underlining key words. All the emphases in the letters I cite are his.

11. *Delphine* was first published, and widely read, in 1802.

12. The allusion to the Trojan War and ravishment suggests that Byron is courting comparison with Helen.

13. Sonia Hofkosh, "Women and the Romantic Author: The Example of Byron," in *Romanticism and Feminism,* ed. Anne K. Mellor (Bloomington: Indiana Univ. Press, 1988), p. 109. Hofkosh is a discerning reader of Byron's fantasies of autonomy and the challenge that women writers and readers pose to them.

14. This feminist reading generally has much to recommend it, but one must always remember that Byron, unlike the other Romantic poets, was not terribly victimized in the marketplace, especially during the years of his greatest fame (1812–16).

15. See also *BLJ* 4:193, 194–95, 196–97. When Byron's engagement to Annabella Milbanke was announced in the Durham newspaper, Lamb wasted no time in contradicting it in the (London) *Morning Chronicle.*

16. Manning, *Byron and His Fictions,* p. 85.

17. In Byron, *His Very Self and Voice: Collected Conversations of Lord Byron,* ed. Ernest J. Lovell, Jr. (New York: Macmillan, 1954), p. 353. Henry Edward Fox was Lord Holland's son, whom Byron met during his years of fame when Fox was an appealing young boy and, like Byron, lame. In March of 1822, he visited Byron in Genoa. After Byron's death, Fox had a love affair with Teresa Guiccioli, subject of chapter 4.

18. Keats's "Isabella" (1820), taken from a story by Boccaccio, presents a woman who squirrels away the head of her murdered lover in a pot of basil and waters it with her tears.

19. Byron's lifelong interest in this story culminated in his translation of it as *Francesca of Rimini* (1820 *CPW* 4:280), a work inspired by his love affair with Teresa Guiccioli.

20. It was no doubt by copying all these letters that Caroline learned Byron's hand.

21. See *BLJ* 3:100. McGann's notes and charts in his edition of the poetry (*CPW*) amply demonstrate how *The Giaour*, as Byron says, "has been lengthening its rattles every month." It encodes Byron's actual role in the rescue of the Turkish woman and his political opinions at the time of the event.

22. *CPW* 3:406; see McGann's illustrative notes on *The Giaour*.

23. See McGann's notes to "Waltz: An Apostrophic Hymn" in *CPW* 3:395.

24. See McGann's notes on the poem's literary and historical background in *CPW* 3:396.

25. Quoted in Marchand, *Byron*, 1:397.

26. Glenarvon, an evil genius in whom Lamb places Byron's saturnine sexiness, is a wonderful waltzer. Lamb's relation to her fictional creature is not unlike Byron's relation both to his (anti)heroes in the oriental tales and to Lamb herself. If Glenarvon is Caroline's Giaour, then Gulnare/Kaled (in *The Corsair / Lara*) is Byron's Caroline. When lovers seek literary images of themselves and use these images to make love and war, they get lost—and sometimes lose us—in the hall of mirrors their fictions construct around them.

27. Both Gulnare and Kaled appear to commemorate and idealize Byron's attachment to Lamb. The cross-dressed Kaled would seem a less threatening version of the virile Gulnare. As a reflection of Lara, Kaled is not even a miniature writ large: she is merely a miniature.

28. Quoted in Malcolm Elwin, *Lord Byron's Wife* (New York: Harcourt, Brace & World, 1962), p. 146.

29. If Caroline's echo of *Purgatorio* is faint, Byron's, in a letter to Teresa Guiccioli dated July 17, 1820, is not: "But as to Sandri—I shall find a way of punishing him. there is a certain . . . ? no?—I feel as if I could hear it. *Ricordati di me che son la Pia*" (*BLJ* 7:131). Perhaps Byron is remembering Lady Caroline even as he plants the allusion in Guiccioli's mind.

30. Baudrillard, *Seduction*, p. 13.

31. For a provocative discussion of Byron and transvestism, see Susan J. Wolfson, "'Their She Condition': Cross-Dressing and the Politics of Gender in *Don Juan*," in *English Literary History* 54, no. 3 (1987).

32. Elwin, *Lord Byron's Wife*, p. 146.

33. Daughter of Frederick Ponsonby, third Earl of Bessborough, and his wife Lady Henrietta Frances Spenser, Caroline married William Lamb in 1805. Her husband, second son of Lord Melbourne, would become prime minister under Queen Victoria. Byron's chastisement of her faithlessness to Lamb is, under the circumstances, one of his more astonishing hyprocrisies.

34. *The Compact Edition of the Oxford English Dictionary*, (1971), s.v. "Public."

35. Lady Caroline Lamb, *Glenarvon*, facsimile ed. (New York: Scholars' Facsimiles and Reprints, 1972), 3:91.

36. One should also remember Byron's remark in a letter to Samuel Rogers (July 29, 1816): "I have read 'Glenarvon.' 'From furious Sappho scarce a milder fate / — — —by her love—or libelled by her hate.'" (*BLJ* 5:86) These lines are an allusion to Pope's *Horace Imitated*, bk. 2, sat. 1, ll. 83–84. Hofkosh writes of the threat *Glenarvon* posed to Byron: "For the poet who repeatedly evaded

admitting the autobiographical resonances of his own work, such a rendering of his personal language in another's text calls the very definition of his authorship *as* personal language into question. *Glenarvon* shows that the author's private life and work are always another's imaginative property" ("Women and the Romantic Author, p. 105).

37. Lamb first experimented with this form in *Gordon: A Tale*, which consists of two cantos of criticism of *Don Juan*.

38. Strickland, *The Byron Women*, p. 60.

39. Bernard Grebanier, *The Uninhibited Byron: An Account of His Sexual Confusion* (New York: Crown, 1970), p. 144.

40. Samuel C. Chew, *Byron in England: His Fame and After-Fame* (New York: Russell & Russell, 1965), p. 51. Lamb could not have read more than Cantos 1 and 2 of *Don Juan* by the summer of 1819. It is not clear why Chew thinks she has read through Canto 12, composed in late 1822.

41. Peter W. Graham, *Don Juan and Regency England*, (Charlottesville: Univ. Of Virginia Press, 1990), pp. 119–20.

42. Caroline Lamb, "A New Canto," reproduced in Strickland, *The Byron Women*, p. 212. Subsequent quotations in the text cite this source parenthetically as *NC*, with page number (neither stanzas nor lines are numbered).

43. In order to avoid this inelegant cluster, I refer hereafter to the ventriloquist Lamb by her name alone and trust that the context will make it clear that I mean "Lamb-as-Byron."

44. The reviewer is Henry Brougham, though Byron thought it was Francis Jeffrey, the chief editor of the *Edinburgh Review*.

45. Byron describes Haidee as "Nature's bride" (*CPW* 5:152).

46. For a passage that seems to have been directly on Caroline's mind, see *CPW* 5:105 ("but at intervals there gush'd, / Accompanied with a convulsive splash, / A solitary shriek, the bubbling cry / Of some strong swimmer in his agony"). The shipwreck sequence is followed by the Haidee episode in *Don Juan*. For the bride of nature's shrieking, see *CPW* 5:214 ("Then shrieking, she arose, and shrieking fell").

47. "Here, in this grotto of the wave-worn shore, / They passed the Tropic's red meridian o'er" (*CPW* 7:46). "They" are Torquil and Neuha, who seem rather to enjoy their damp and drizzly love nest.

48. Byron wrote that Blackwood was Murray's "brother Bibliopole in Edinburgh" (*BLJ* 3:238).

49. In Lamb's stanza five, for example:

> The roaring streamers flap, red flakes are shot
> This way and that, the town is a volcano—
> And yells are heard, like those provoked by Lot,
> Some, of the Smithfield sort, and some *soprano*;
> Some holy water seek, the font is hot,
> And fizzing in a tea-kettle *piano*.

Now brings your magistrates, with yeomen back'd,
Bawls Belial, and read the Riot-Act!—

50. For Byron's droll response to this incident, see *BLJ* 7:169.

3. THE DIVINING OF BYRON

1. For the sake of consistency, throughout this chapter I refer to Annabella Milbanke by her maiden name (with only the occasional bow to "Lady Byron").

2. These unpublished poems may be found in the British Library. I am indebted to Jerome McGann for making facsimiles of them available to me. As far as I know, they have never been critically treated.

3. Quoted in Ethel Colburn Mayne, *The Life and Letters of Anne Isabella, Lady Noel Byron* (New York: Scribner, 1929), p. 12 (the ellipses are Mayne's).

4. Quoted in ibid., p. 13.

5. Quoted in Marchand, *Byron*, 1:338. The following eruption (dated November 17, 1811) also suggests the nature of Byron's feeling toward Milbanke's poetry and toward women writers in general: "I have heard nothing of Miss Milbanke's posthumous buffooneries, but here is Miss Seward with 6 tomes of the most disgusting trash, sailing over Styx with a Foolscap over her periwig as complacent as can be.—Of all Bitches dead or alive a scribbling woman is the most canine" (*BLJ* 2:132).

6. Mayne, *Life*, p. 13.

7. Ibid., p. 44.

8. About two years later (March 15, 1814), Byron wrote to Milbanke: "To rob you of my conversion some pious person has written & is about to publish a long poem—an 'Anti-Byron' which he sent to Murray—who (not very fairly) sent it to me—and I advised him to print it—but some strange sort of bookselling delicacy won't let him—however some one else will" (*BLJ* 4:82).

9. Harriet Beecher Stowe, *Lady Byron Vindicated* (London: Sampson, Low, Sini, and Marston, 1870), p. 393. Stowe makes good her radical anti-Byromania throughout her vindication of Lady Byron. This enterprise usually involves making Annabella into a perfect saint, Byron into a perfect devil.

10. Mayne, *Life*, p. 37.

11. Ibid., p. 124.

12. Quoted in ibid., p. 70. (One recalls the maxim of La Rouchefoucauld, "There are those who would never be in love had they never heard the word love.")

13. Quoted in Mayne, *Life*, p. 37.

14. Quoted in Elwin, *Lord Byron's Wife*, p. 258. In this daisy-chain of literary narcissism, one must note that Edward Trelawney in turn modeled himself on Byron's Lara; in fact he allegedly slept with a copy of the poem under his pillow.

15. Ibid.

16. McGann suggests two other possible recipients, Lady Adelaide Forbes and Miss Mercer Elphinstone. See *CPW* 3:424.

17. "I am glad you like 'the Corsair' which they tell me is popular" (*BLJ* 4:56).

18. I am indebted to Jerome McGann for this deciphering.

19. The relevant biblical texts here are Isaiah 42:3 and Matthew 12:20: "A bruised reed shall not he break."

20. Quoted in Mayne, *Life*, p. 124.

21. I would argue that as Byron's popularity soared, he found it increasingly difficult to separate himself from the titanically sullen antiheroes he represented in his tales. As his own "image man," he had to take some responsibility for his fictional creatures, and though he seemed loath to do so, he clearly enjoyed all the games of referential cat-and-mouse his tales generated. Beginning with the third and fourth cantos of *Childe Harold's Pilgrimage*, Byron stopped flinching, and the more he revealed about himself and his views—especially in the early cantos of *Don Juan*—the more his English readers grew to despise him. For he was no longer writing exotic, innocuous fictions. He was editing their hypocrisies.

22. See McGann's notes to the poem in *CPW* 3:431–35.

23. Mayne, *Life*, pp. 51–52.

24. George Eden had proposed to Annabella in 1810 and was rejected. See Elwin, *Lord Byron's Wife*, pp. 92–94.

25. A longer discussion of Byron's alternately serious and facetious attitudes about his own redemption would include an analysis of *Cain* as a drama pitting human love (Annabella as Adah) against demonic knowledge.

26. More troubled-water imagery appears in Byron's most famous poem about his love for Teresa, "Stanzas to the Po," written in early June of 1819 when Teresa was suddenly forced to go with her husband to Ravenna. The poem shows Byron ambivalent about this latest love affair. He deflects his anxieties about their separation onto the River Po, which serves as an artery symbolically connecting him to Teresa, whom he believes to be at Ca'Zen, near the mouth of the Po. Many lines in the poem recall Annabella's "What eye can search the ocean deep," especially

> What if thy deep and ample stream should be
> A mirror of my heart, where she may read
> The thousand thoughts I now betray to thee
> Wild as thy wave and headlong as thy speed?

27. McGann's notes in *CPW* 3:466 suggest that it was in fact written at Hanalby in Jan. 1815, which would date it about the time Annabella was writing her own surging melodies.

28. Jean Hagstrum, *Eros and Vision: The Restoration to Romanticism* (Evanston, Ill: Northwestern Univ. Press, 1989), p. 181.

29. Quoted in Elwin, *Lord Byron's Wife*, p. 284. It is not clear to whom Annabella recalled this observation.

30. Peter Quennell, *Byron: The Years of Fame* (Hamden: Archon Books, 1967), pp. 208–9.

31. The epigram that forms a caption to this illustration appears in Byron's "Stanzas" (1811; see *CPW* 1:349–50):

Away, away, ye notes of woe!
　Be silent thou once soothing strain,
Or I must flee from hence, for, oh!
　I dare not trust those sounds again.

To me they speak of brighter days:
　But lull the chords, for now, alas!
I must not think, I may not gaze
　On what I am, on what I was.

The voice that made those sounds more sweet
　Is hush'd, and all their charms are fled;
And now their softest notes repeat,
　A dirge, an anthem o'er the dead!

Yes, Thyrza! yes, they breathe of thee,
　Beloved dust! since dust thou art;
And all that once was harmony
　Is worse than discord to my heart!

'Tis silent all!—but on my ear
　The well-remember'd echoes thrill;
I hear a voice I would not hear,
　A voice that now might well be still.

Yet oft my doubting soul 'twill shake:
　Ev'n slumber owns its gentle tone,
Till consciousness will vainly wake
　To listen, though the dream be flown.

Sweet Thyrza! waking as in sleep,
　Thou art but now a lovely dream;
A star that trembl'd o'er the deep,
　Then turn'd from earth its tender beam.

But he, who through life's dreary way
　Must pass, when heav'n is veil'd in wrath,
Will long lament the vanish'd ray
　That scatter'd gladness o'er his path.

32. The Heath engraving was based on a Stothard drawing; see Shelley M. Bennett, *Thomas Stothard: The Mechanisms of Art Patronage in England circa 1800* (Columbia: Univ. Of Missouri Press, 1988), pp. 80–81, for notes on the

twelve illustrations by Stothard that Murray commissioned for the 1815 edition of Byron's works.

33. Quoted in Leslie Marchand, "'Come to me, my adored boy, George': Byron's Ordeal with Lady Falkland," in *Byron Journal* 16 (1988): 23. Christina, Lady Falkland, was the widow of Byron's friend Lord Falkland, who was killed in a duel. Out of generosity Byron had a few years earlier left Lady Falkland a substantial sum of money in a teacup. As soon as he became famous, she became one of the more visibly infatuated ladies of Regency Society.

34. Louis Crompton, *Byron and Greek Love: Homophobia in 19th-Century England* (Berkeley: Univ. of California Press, 1985), p. 194.

35. In Appendix B of *Astarte*, Ralph Milbanke, Lord Lovelace, prints this poem but does not include a date. Byron wrote it in early May 1814, but it was not published until Isaac Nathan brought out a revised edition of *A Selection of Hebrew Melodies* (1827–29).

36. See Ralph Milbanke, *Astarte*, p. 162.

37. Quoted in Charles du Bos, *Byron and the Need of Fatality*, trans. E.C. Mayne (New York: Haskell House, 1970), p. 284.

38. At the conclusion of *Byron and the Need of Fatality*, du Bos offers a painfully sentimental account in which he has Byron on his deathbed cry out for Annabella as his confessor, a role she cherished during their marriage. The scene, as du Bos recounts it, has pronounced affinities with Manfred's feckless and histrionic pleas for forgiveness. Here we have yet another demonstration that male as well as female critics and biographers embalm Byron and posthumously give birth to the very "Byron" Annabella wished to recreate during their courtship.

39. Quoted in McGann's notes to the poem (no. 243) in *CPW* 3:462.

40. I am thinking of the apocryphal stories about Byron's sodomizing Annabella on their wedding night. If they are true, such behavior could be interpreted as his savage re-Pygmalionizing of the woman who had trapped him in monogamy and heterosexuality. In treating her like a Greek boy, he would reassert his authority and fierce unconventionality—his will not to be cast in the mold of "Lord Annabella."

41. See Ione Dodson Young, *A Concordance to the Poetry of Byron* (Austin, Best, 1965). This poem was first correctly attributed to Lady Byron in *CPW* 1, at the end of the editorial introduction.

42. Marchand, *Byron*, 2:562.

43. See McGann's commentary to *Manfred* in *CPW* 4:463.

44. I do not agree with Philip Martin (*Byron*, p. 133) that *Manfred* is merely "absurdly eclectic," or that it is "an aggressive but nonchalantly cheerful response to Byron's dilemma." I am arguing that it is a devious, vexed response to his dilemma, a hate poem "staging" his animosity.

45. Quoted in Malcom Elwin, *Lord Byron's Family* (London: John Murray, 1975) p. 147.

46. Mario Praz, *The Romantic Agony* (London: Oxford Univ. Press, 1933), p. 73.

4. UNWRITING HIS BODY

1. Bernard Blackstone, *Byron: A Survey* (London, Longman, 1975), p. 301.

2. Paglia, *Sexual Personae*, p. 359.

3. Cf. also letter of Aug. 3, 1820 (*BLJ* 7:148).

4. Also quoted in Iris Origo, *The Last Attachment*, (New York: Charles Scribners Sons, 1949), p. 163.

5. Quoted in ibid., p. 113. The passage appears on page 81 of Madame de Staël's *Corinne* (Paris: Libra vie Garrier Frères, 1807).

6. Quoted in Origo, *The Last Attachment*, p. 113.

7. Quoted in ibid., p. 213.

8. Ibid.

9. Another case in point: on June 15, 1819, Byron wrote Teresa: "My Soul: I speak of *Love* and you and you answer me about [The Lament of] *Tasso.* I write about *you*, and you ask me about '*Eleanora.*' If you want to render me even more insane than he is, I can assure you are on the way to succeeding."

10. Quoted in Origo, *The Last Attachment*, p. 214.

11. Ibid., p. 71

12. Ibid., p. 76.

13. Ibid.

14. *Petrarch's Lyric Poems*, trans. and ed. Robert M. Durling (Cambridge: Harvard Univ. Press, 1976), p. 242.

15. "To the Po" flows into Byron's other "river" poem to Teresa "[Stanzas ('Could love for ever')]," which recounts his even more tumultuous anxiety about being separated from her the following December. After Byron's death Teresa produced two fragmented transcripts of this poem to send to Thomas Moore. See McGann's notes in *CPW* 1:505.

16. Origo, *The Last Attachment*, p. 73.

17. This is John D. Sinclair's translation of Dante's *Inferno* (New York: Oxford Univ. Press, 1961) p. 79.

18. "His Byronic Muse procured for him the hand of one our fair country-women [Annabella]," *Blackwoods Magazine* 13 (1823): 51. In attacking Fanny Silvestrini (a go-between for Byron and Teresa for a short period), Byron wrote Teresa: "Fanny's letter is a portrait of 'the procuress who wrote it'" (*BLJ* 7:209). One needs a scorecard to mark off all the procurers.

19. Teresa went through her copy of Thomas Moore's *Life* and scratched out the word "amor" in reference to her, and wrote in "amica." She was not the first woman whom Byron fancied a Francesca to his Paolo. Of his tempestuous affair with Caroline Lamb, he wrote to Lady Melbourne: "I beg to be spared from meeting her until we may be chained together in Dante's *Inferno*" (*BLJ* 3:36). And in 1819 he wrote to his half-sister, Augusta Leigh, about their illicit love: "It is heart-breaking to think of our long Separation—and I am sure more than punishment enough for all our sins—Dante is more humane in his 'hell' for he places his unfortunate lovers (Francesca of Rimini & Paolo whose case fell a good deal short of *ours*—though sufficiently naughty) in company—and though they suffer—it is at least together" (*BLJ* 3:129).

20. See the preface to *The Corsair* (*CPW* 3:149–50).

21. Quoted in Donald Reiman, *Shelley and His Circle*, (Cambridge: Harvard Univ. Press, 1976), 8:419.

22. The term is his, from *Beppo*, l. 315. "Lord Byron," wrote Guiccioli in *La Vie de Lord Byron en Italie*, "began to play his role [of *cavalier servente*] with pleasure, indeed, but not without laughing at it a little. . . . One would almost have thought that he was a little ashamed—that in showing himself kind he was making an avowal of weakness and being deficient in that virility of soul which he admired so much. . . . This was a great fault of Lord Byron's" (quoted in Origo, *The Last Attachment*, p. 147).

23. Countess Teresa Guiccioli, *My Recollections of Lord Byron*, trans. Hubert E.H. Jerginham (Philadelphia, 1869), 1:1.

24. Ibid., 1:6.

25. In *A Love's Eye View* (Salzburg: Institut für Anglistik und Amerikanistik, 1988), Edwin A. Stürzl closely examines the text of *La Vie de Lord Byron en Italie* in order "to compare the portrait she offers with that presented by current critical Byron biographies, so that a judgment may be passed on the Countess's reliability and objectivity." This way of thinking of biography seems pointlessly positivistic, particularly in the case of Byron and the constructors and purveyors of his legend, all of whom seem caught up in a grand game of illusions, allusions, public and private images, and personal fantasy. Stürzl's stated intention does not seem to follow from the generous spirit of his title, which points up Teresa's thoroughly subjective perspective.

26. Guiccioli, *Recollections*, 1:30.

27. Guiccioli's editing is her way of rewriting Byron's play *The Deformed Transformed* (1822).

28. On Sept. 11, 1823, Pietro Gamba wrote to his sister Teresa: "What spectres have been called up by your diseased imagination" (quoted in Origo, *The Last Attachment*, p. 362). See also *BLJ* 2:53, 6:158.

29. Guiccioli, *Recollections*, 1:425.

30. "The women hate everything which strips off the tinsel of *Sentiment*—& they are right—or it would rob them of their weapons" (*BLJ* 7:202).

31. Paul West, *The Spoiler's Art* (New York: St. Martin's Press, 1960), p. 14.

32. Guiccioli, *Recollections*, 1:448.

33. Ibid.

34. See *BLJ* 1:122–23.

35. Guiccioli, *Recollections* 1:453.

36. Ibid., 1:454–55.

37. Ibid., p. 117.

38. Mary Shelley's stake in enshrining her husband parallels Teresa's spiritualizing of Byron. One might think of Mary's careful editing of Percy's works with an eye to his apotheosis as her attempt to reanimate the corpus of her dead husband, to produce a beautiful creature, and herself play the part of a responsible, caring creator.

39. Guiccioli, *Recollections*, 1:437

40. Alex Owen, *The Darkened Room: Women, Power, and Spiritualism in Late Victorian England* (London: Virago Press, 1989), pp. 6, 12.

41. See Stürzl, *A Love's Eye View.*

42. Whether Teresa's books of automatic writing have survived remains a mystery. I have been searching for them for five years.

43. Mary R. Darby-Smith, "My Reminiscences of Madame la Marquise de Boissey," *Victoria Magazine*, Nov. 1873.

44. Ibid., p. 6.

45. Ibid., pp. 12–13.

46. Ibid., p. 14.

47. Ibid., p. 15.

48. Scott, *Letters on Demonology*, p. 87.

49. Guiccioli, *Vie*, 1:47.

5. THE ART OF CONVERSATION

1. In a letter of Nov. 11, 1804, Byron's comment to Augusta Byron about his mother's dreadful scoldings suggests an early contempt for female vociferousness: "Her words are of that rough texture, which offend more than personal ill usage. 'A talkative woman is like an Adder's tongue,' so says one of the prophets" (*BLJ* 1:55–56). Perhaps his mother's tongue-lashings marked him and his views of women for life.

2. Marguerite Blessington, *The Idler in Italy*, 1:389.

3. It is worth mentioning that the Blessingtons, as Doris Langley Moore writes, "put aside grief for the[ir] dead infant to inveigle the living celebrity" (*The Late Lord Byron*, p. 470).

4. This volume, a sextodecimo of 97 pages, represents a distillation of Blessington's two-volume "Night Thoughts Book," which bulks out at 319 pages.

5. This is also the year Blessington published "Thoughts on Byron Suggested by a Picture Representing His Contemplation of the Coliseum," *Keepsake*, pp. 180–83.

6. Quoted in Lovell's introduction to *Lady Blessington's Conversations of Lord Byron* (Princeton: Princeton Univ. Press, 1969), p. 40.

7. Blessington, *Desultory Thoughts and Reflections* (New York: Wiley and Putnam, 1839; hereafter cited as *DTR*).

8. Quoted in Doris Langley Moore, *The Late Lord Byron*, p. 481.

9. Ibid., p. 480.

10. Leslie A. Marchand, *Byron's Poetry: A Critical Introduction* (Boston: Houghton Mifflin, 1965), p. 248.

11. Quoted in Lovell's introduction to Blessington, *Conversations*, p. 91.

12. Blessington, Conversations, p. 155.

13. Blessington, *DTR*, p. 54.

14. Ibid., p. 66.

15. Quoted in Origo, *The Last Attachment*, p. 341, citing Guiccioli, *Vie*, pp. 1491–1500: "Lady Blessington avait beaucoup d'imagination et une presque nécessité de faire un roman de la plus simple histore. . . . On les a appellée imaginaires et elles le sont en réalité, ces conversations qui trahissent dans l'auteur un secret sentiment de dépit et de malaise."

16. Byron expressly, if playfully, twice says this. First, in some inpromptu lines he gave her:

> Beneath Blessington's eyes
> The reclaimed Paradise
> Should be free as the former from evil;
> But if the new Eve
> For an Apple should grieve,
> What mortal would not play the devil?

And second, in an offer to accompany her to a masked ball: "As someone must play the devil, I will do it" (quoted in Lovell's Introduction, p. 44).

17. Blessington, *Conversations*, p. 20.

18. Preface to ibid., p. 3.

19. Quoted in James A. Clifford, *Hester Lynch Piozzi* (Oxford: Clarendon Press, 1941), p. 262.

20. Horace Walpole, *Letters*, ed. Charles Duke Yonge (London: Unwin, 1891) 1:xiii, 337.

21. Clifford, *Hester Lynch Piozzi*, p. 259.

22. Quoted in ibid., p. 264.

23. Leo Braudy, *The Frenzy of Renown* (Oxford: Oxford Univ. Press 1986), p. 407.

24. Ibid., p. 382.

25. Lovell, introduction to Blessington, *Conversations*, p. 92.

26. They are, chronologically, as follows: R.C. Dállas, *Recollections of the Life of Lord Byron, from the Year 1808 to the End of 1814* (1824); Thomas Medwin, *Conversations of Lord Byron: Noted during a Residence with His Lordship at Pisa, in the Years 1821 and 1822* (1824); Pietro Gamba, *A Narrative of Lord Byron's Last Journey to Greece* (1825); William Parry, *The Last Days of Lord Byron* (1825); Leigh Hunt, *Lord Byron and Some of His Contemporaries* (1828); Leicester Stanhope, *Greece in 1823, 1824* (1825); James Kennedy, *Conversations of Religion, with Lord Byron and Others, Held in Cephalonia* (1830); Isaac Nathan, *Fugitive Pieces and Reminiscences of Lord Byron* (1829); John Galt, *The Life of Lord Byron* (1830); Thomas Moore, *Letters and Journal of Lord Byron, with Notices of His Life* (1830); Julius Milligen, *Memoirs of the Affairs of Greece* (1831).

27. Quoted by Lovell, in Byron, *His Very Self and Voice*, xxiii–xxv.

28. Lovell's editions of Medwin's and Blessington's conversations with Byron form two impressively expanded footnotes to his own great contribution to Byron studies and the Byron legend, the compendious *His Very Self and Voice: Collected Conversations of Lord Byron*. My own work on the Byron

legend and its curators suggests that the interplay of images, poems, and voices involved in creating and sustaining this legend is too complex for any one's "very self" to emerge.

29. Quoted in R.R. Madden, *The Literary Life and Correspondence of the Countess Blessington* (London: T.C. Newby,1855), 1:276.

30. Ibid.

31. Blessington, *Conversations*, p. 5.

32. Quoted in Madden, *Literary Life*, p. 83. One of her "Night Thoughts" shows us a chastened Marguerite: "The world is given to indulge in the very erroneous supposition that there exists an identity between the writings of authors and their actual lives and characters."

33. Blessington, *Conversations*, p. 110.

34. Blessington, *DTR*, p. 43

35. Patricia Meyer Spacks, *Gossip* (New York: Knopf, 1985), p. 101.

36. Quoted in Lovell, introduction to Blessington, *Conversations*, p. 88.

37. Ibid.

38. Speaking of the society in which she moved, Blessington referred to "the modern Babylon . . . where thinking and feeling are almost unknown" (quoted in J. Fitzgerald Molloy, *The Most Gorgeous Lady Blessington*, [New York: Scribner's, 1896], p. 227).

39. Blessington, *Conversations.*, pp. 40–41.

40. Doris Langley Moore, *The Late Lord Byron*, p. 477.

41. Blessington, *Conversations*, p. 42.

42. Ibid.

43. Clearly, Blessington dipped her pen in vinegar when she referred to Byron as a child: "Byron is, after all, a spoiled child" (*Conversations*, p. 54); "[he] is like a spoiled child who finds he cannot have everything his own way" (p. 83). This sort of patronizing treatment, along with her condescending refrain, "Poor Byron," makes her appear to be his superior. Remarking Byron's childishness also punctures the commonplace of the childlike Romantic artist. Like Peter Shaffer's Mozart in *Amadeus*, Blessington's Byron shows us the infantile side of his genius.

44. Late in the *Conversations*, Blessington paused to defend her presentation of Byron's full disclosures. She wrote that his confessions "were not confided with any injunction to secrecy, but were indiscriminately made to his chance companions." Medwin, in the preface to his *Conversations* said of Byron's disclosures to him, "They were communicated . . . without any injunction to secrecy." Blessington echoed Medwin's defense in order to cite precedent for her project, then claimed that Byron "often declared his decided intention of writing copious notes to the Life [i.e., his memoirs] he had given to [Thomas] Moore, in which *the whole truth* should be declared of, for, and against himself and others." If Byron was completely indiscriminate in his disclosures, why should his auditors be any less so in reporting them?

45. Blessington, *Conversations*, p. 152.

46. Ibid. (original emphasis).

47. Thomas Moore, *Letters and Journals of Lord Byron,* 1:25–26.

48. In January 1813, Caroline Lamb went so far as to engrave and publicize this lack of trust. Informing Lady Melbourne of Lamb's prank, Byron wrote: She [Lady Caroline] is perfectly at liberty . . . to put whatever motto she may devise on her *'livery buttons'* this last she will understand but as you probably may not—it is as well to say that one of her amusements by her own account has been engraving on the said 'buttons' *Ne* "Crede Byron" an interesting addition to the motto of my family which thus atones for it's [sic] degradation in my acquaintance with her"(*BLJ* 3:9).

49. Blessington, *Conversations,* p. 152.

50. See *CPW* 5:635, stanzas 51–52.

51. One of Blessington's most hauntingly beautiful entries in *DTR* is under the heading, "Presentiments": "Presentiments are the heart's prophecies; for the heart is a sibyl deeply skilled in all the mysteries of her own realm."

52. Blessington, *Conversations,* p. 80. Lovell's splendid introduction to this edition contains a wealth of information about Lady Blessington's background and the circumstances leading up to and following her interviews with Byron; his footnotes also show how heavily Blessington relied on Medwin's *Conversations,* which form something like the scaffolding for the construction of her published work. I am indebted to his scholarly industry and attempt here only to make a case for the complexity and richness of Blessington's secret identification with her subject.

53. Blessington, *Conversations,* p. 85.

54. In the front of her copy of the *Conversations,* Guiccioli wrote her claim that Byron had said to her, "C'est un caractere que j'etudie pour Don Juan (Ly Adeline)."

55. Blessington, *Conversations,* p. 47.

56. Ibid., p. 71.

57. See *CPW* 5:769 n. 820 (original emphasis).

58. Michael Cooke, *Acts of Inclusion: Studies Bearing on an Elementary Theory of Romanticism* (New Haven: Yale Univ. Press, 1979), p. 226.

59. Blessington, *Conversations,* p. 153.

60. Quoted in Madden, *Literary Life,* 1:284–85.

61. Quoted in Lovell's introduction to Blessington, *Conversations,* p. 90.

62. Madden, *Literary Life,* 1:205.

63. Blessington, *DTR,* p. 10.

64. Blessington, *Conversations,* p. 83.

65. In her copy of the *Conversations,* at a point where Byron had been wistfully referring to his avarice, Guiccioli wrote in the margins: "Mystification que tout cela! ou inventions!" (Lovell presents Guiccioli's marginalia in footnotes to his edition of Blessington, *Conversations;* see p. 182). We thus can see how Guiccioli edited Blessington's fantasy recollections, just as she would later edit Byron's poetry to present their love affair in the most glamorous light.

66. Quoted in Elwin, *Lord Byron's Family,* p. 175.

67. See Jerome J. McGann, "Lord Byron's Twin Opposites of Truth," in *Towards a Literature of Knowledge* (Oxford: Clarendon Press, 1989), esp. pp. 40–43.

68. Blessington's concern for reading Byron's face like an open book indicates her interest in what Leo Braudy (*Frenzy of Renown*, p. 402) calls "a European craze for physiognomy," a quasi-scientific fetish for analyzing faces that gained momentum from a treatise by Johann Kaspar Lavater (1775–78), who "tried to create a 'science' of the face and its expressions by which character might be read directly."

69. Blessington, *Conversations*, p. 81.

70. Ibid.

71. Ibid.

72. Ibid., pp. 81–82.

73. Ibid., p. 116.

74. *CPW* 3:213; see Chapter 3 for the entire passage. Blessington's use of this passage to analyze Byron's character is a particularly ingrown plagiarism, since he partly invented the poetic terms and images she later used to describe him.

75. Blessington, *DTR*, pp. 82–83.

76. Paul de Man, *The Rhetoric of Romanticism* (New York: Columbia Univ. Press, 1984), p. 70.

77. Ibid.

78. Blessington, *Conversations*, p. 162.

79. Ibid., p. 162.

80. Ibid., p. 163.

81. Ibid., p. 107.

82. Ibid.

83. Quoted by Lovell in Blessington, *Conversations*, p. 89.

84. Blessington, *DTR*, p. 17.

APPENDIX B

1. See esp. Paul West, *Lord Byron's Doctor* (New York: Doubleday, 1989), pp. 25–26 and passim for a comic, if dire, depiction of the fictionalized Polidori succumbing to the allure of his patient.

2. Amanda Prantera, *Conversations with Lord Byron on Perversion, 163 Years after His Lordship's Death* (London, Cape, 1987), pp. 24–25. Subsequent references to the novel are cited by page number in the text.

3. I suspect that the ULBL is a thinly veiled reference to an actual organization, the International Byron Society.

4. Hagstrum, *Eros and Vision*, p. 181.

5. Louis Crompton, *Byron and Greek Love* (Berkeley: Univ. of California Press, 1985). See especially chaps. 2, 3, and 4.

6. Quoted in Elwin, *Lord Byron's Wife*, p. 284.

Selected Bibliography

PRIMARY TEXTS

Blessington, Marguerite. *Desultory Thoughts and Reflections.* New York: Wiley and Putnam, 1839.

———. *Lady Blessington's Conversations of Lord Byron.* Ed. Ernest J. Lovell Jr. Princeton: Princton Univ. Press, 1969.

———. *The Idler in Italy.* 2 vols. London: Henry Colburn, 1839.

Byron, George Gordon, Lord. *Byron's Letters and Journals.* Ed. Leslie A. Marchand. 12 vols. Cambridge: Harvard Univ. Press, 1973–82.

———. *His Very Self and Voice: Collected Conversations of Lord Byron.* Ed. Ernest J. Lovell Jr. New York: Macmillan, 1954.

———. *Lord Byron's Correspondence.* Ed. John Murray. 2 vols. London: John Murray, 1922.

———. *Lord Byron: The Complete Poetical Works.* Ed. Jerome J. McGann. 7 vols. Oxford: Clarendon Press, 1980–92.

———. *The Works of Lord Byron: Letters and Journals.* Ed. John Murray and R.E. Prothero. 6 vols. London: John Murray, 1898–1901.

———. *Byron's Don Juan: A Variorum Edition.* Ed. T.G. Steffan and W.W. Pratt. 4 vols. 2d ed. Austin: Univ. of Texas Press, 1971.

Guiccioli, Teresa. *My Recollections of Lord Byron.* 2 pts. Trans. Hubert E.H. Jerginham. London: Bentley, 1869.

———. *La Vie de Lord Byron en Italie.* Ed. Erwin A. Sthrzl. Salzburg: Institut für Anglistik und Amerikanistik, 1983.

Lamb, Caroline. *Glenarvon.* Delmar: Scholars' Facsimiles & Reprints, 1972.

Medwin, Thomas. *"Conversations of Lord Byron."* Ed. Ernest J. Lovell Jr. Princeton: Princeton Univ. Press, 1966.

Milbanke, Ralph, Earl of Lovelace. *Astarte: A Fragment of Truth concerning George Gordon, Sixth Lord Byron.* London: Christophers, 1921.

Origo, Iris. *The Last Attachment.* New York: Scribner's Sons, 1949.

"To Lord Byron": Feminine Profiles Based upon Unpublished Letters, 1807–1824. Ed. George Paston and Peter Quennell. New York: Scribner's Sons, 1939.

Young, Ione Dodson, ed. *A Concordance to the Poetry of Byron.* 4 vols. Austin: Pemberton Press, 1965.

SECONDARY TEXTS

Baudrillard, Jean. *Seduction.* New York: St. Martin's Press, 1990.
Bennett, Shelley M. *Thomas Stothard: The Mechanisms of Art Patronage in England circa 1800.* Columbia: Longman, 1988.
Blackstone, Bernard. *Byron: A Survey.* London: Longman, 1975.
Boyes, Megan. *Love without Wings: A biography of Elizabeth Pigot.* Derby: J.M. Tatler & Son, 1988.
Braudy, Leo. *The Frenzy of Renown.* Oxford: Oxford Univ. Press, 1986.
Chew, Samuel C. *Byron In England, His Fame and After-Fame.* New York: Russell & Russell, 1965.
Christensen, Jerome. *Lord Byron's Strength.* Baltimore: Johns Hopkins Univ. Press, 1994.
Cooke, Michael G. *Acts of Inclusion: Studies Bearing on an Elementary Theory of Romanticism.* New Haven: Yale Univ. Press, 1979.
Crompton, Louis. *Byron and Greek Love: Homophobia in 19th-Century England.* Berkeley: Univ. of California Press, 1985.
du Bos, Charles. *Byron and the Need of Fatality.* Trans. Ethel C. Mayne. New York: Haskell House, 1970.
Elwin, Malcolm. *Lord Byron's Family.* London: John Murray, 1975.
———. *Lord Byron's Wife.* New York: Harcourt, Brace & World, 1962.
Franklin, Caroline. *Byron's Heroines.* Oxford: Clarendon Press. 1992.
Gleckner, Robert F. *Critical Essays on Lord Byron.* New York: G.K. Hall, 1991.
Graham, Peter W. *Don Juan and Regency Society.* Charlottesville: Univ. of Virginia Press, 1990.
Gray, Austin K. *Teresa; Or Her Demon Lover.* London: G.G. Harrap, 1948.
Grenbanier, Bernard. *The Uninhibited Byron: An Account of His Sexual Confusion.* New York: Crown, 1970.
Hagstrum, Jean. *Eros and Vision: The Restoration to Romanticism.* Evanston, Ill.: Northwestern Univ. Press, 1989.
Lang, Cecil. "Narcissus Jilted: Byron and the Biographical Imperative." In *Historical Studies and Literary Criticism,* ed. Jerome J. McGann. Madison: Univ. of Wisconsin Press, 1985.
Levine, Alice. *Rereading Byron: Essays Selected from Hofstra University's Byron Bicentennial Conference.* New York: Garland, 1988.
McGann, Jerome J. *Don Juan in Context.* Chicago: Univ. of Chicago Press, 1976.

———. *Fiery Dust: Byron's Poetic Development.* Chicago: Univ. of Chicago Press, 1968.

Madden, R.R. *The Literary Life and Correspondence of the Countess of Blessington.* London: T.C. Newby, 1855.

Manning, Peter J. *Byron and His Fictions.* Detroit: Wayne State Univ. Press, 1978.

Marchand, Leslie. *Byron: A Biography.* 3 vols. New York: Knopf, 1957.

Martin, Philip W. *Byron: A Poet before His Public.* Cambridge: Cambridge Univ. Press, 1982.

Mayne, Ethel Colburn. *Enchanters of Men.* New York: Methuen, 1905.

———. *The Life and Letters of Anne Isabella, Lady Noel Byron.* New York: Scribner, 1929.

Molloy, J. Fitzgerald. *The Most Gorgeous Lady Blessington.* New York: Scribner, 1896.

Moore, Doris Langley. *The Late Lord Byron.* London: John Murray, 1961.

Paglia, Camille. *Sexual Personae: Art and Decadence from Nefertiti to Emily Dickinson.* New Haven: Yale Univ. Press, 1990.

Pratt, Willis. *Byron at Southwell.* Austin: Univ. of Texas Press, 1948.

Praz, Mario *The Romantic Agony.* London: Oxford Univ. Press, 1933.

Reiman, Donald. *Shelley and His Circle.* Cambridge: Harvard Univ. Press, 1976.

Scott, Sir Walter. *Letters on Demonology and Witchcraft.* 2d ed. New York: J. & J. Harper, 1831.

Spacks, Patricia. *Gossip.* Chicago: Univ. of Chicago Press, 1985.

Stowe, Harriet Beecher. *Lady Byron Vindicated.* London: Sampson, Low, Son, and Marston, 1870.

Strickland, Margot. *The Byron Women.* London: Peter Owen, 1974.

Walsh, George B. *The Varieties of Enchantment: Early Greek Views of the Nature and Function of Poetry.* Chapel Hill: Univ. of North Carolina Press, 1984.

West, Paul. *The Spoiler's Art.* New York: St. Martin's Press, 1960.

Index